THE PRESIDENT'S JOURNEY

Issues and Ideals in the Community College

Cathryn L. Addy
Tunxis Community-Technical College

Foreword by George A. Baker III

Anker Publishing Company, Inc.
Bolton, MA

THE PRESIDENT'S JOURNEY

Issues and Ideals in the Community College

ISBN 1-882982-04-5

Compostion by Delphinus, Inc.
Cover design by Deerfoot Studios.

Anker Publishing Company, Inc.
176 Ballville Road
P.O. Box 249
Bolton, MA 01740-0249

ABOUT THE AUTHOR

Cathryn L. Addy is President of Tunxis Community-Technical College in Farmington, Connecticut. She received a B.A (1967) in English from Kansas State University, an M.A. (1971) in English from SUNY-Oswego, and a Ph.D. (1983) from the University of Texas.

Prior to her presidency of Tunxis Community-Technical College, Addy held a number of other teaching and administrative positions. As an English instructor at Auburn Community College in upstate New York, she was nominated by students to receive the Chancellor's Award for Excellence in Teaching. Following advanced graduate studies in English, Addy became interested in counseling and student services. She moved to Central Wyoming College in Riverton, Wyoming to a position as a counselor and advanced quickly to Acting Dean of Student Services and then to the position of Dean of Student Services.

After completing her doctorate, Addy became the founding director of the North Campus of Williamsport Area Community College in Williamsport, Pennsylvania. In 1985, she was named Director of Education for the Art Institute of Philadelphia. In 1987, she was appointed president of Berkshire Community College in Pittsfield, Massachusetts, where she remained as president until assuming the presidency of Tunxis Community-Technical College.

Addy has also served as president of the American Association of Community Colleges President's Academy and was representative to the Executive Committee from the northeast region. In 1990 she received the Distinguished Graduate Award from the University of Texas College of Education for her "national contribution to American community colleges."

CONTENTS

FOREWORD

I'll never forget the day that I met Cathryn Addy. It was the fall of 1981, and she was enrolled in the Community College Leadership Program at the University of Texas at Austin. She was part of a cohort of nineteen graduate students who sought entry into the "club." The "club" consisted of a large number of community college leaders who had graduated from the CCLP since 1944 and had gone on to help community colleges find a place in American higher education.

Not all in her class made it into the "club," but among those who did are directors of other organizations, campus directors, community college administrators, a community college president, and a chancellor of a community college district. Cathryn is unique among this group because she taught in one community college; became a counselor in another; served as dean of student services, campus director, and academic dean at a private school; and President of Berkshire Community College in Massachusetts before accepting a position as President of Tunxis Community-Technical College in Farmington, Connecticut. I believe George Vaughan when he says that the pathway to the presidency is through the academic side of the house. But I always worry about such perceptions becoming guideposts for selection committees and not just one indicator for consideration. My experience tells me that experiential factors may get you an interview, but it is personality, vision, and communication skills that eventually secure the job. Cathryn had the communication skills of an English teacher, the student-centeredness of a counselor, and a leadership style that demonstrated high expectations and true consideration of others.

This book is Cathryn's personal journey into leadership from the executive level. It is a book written by community college leaders for community college leaders. I recommend it to *all* aspiring educational leaders. Universities, colleges, and high schools are all organizations whose primary reason for being is to change people by empowering them to become lifelong learners and to contribute to society. Each organization establishes a unique culture but in the same "petri dish."

In Part One of this book, Cathryn Addy and her contributors deal with such topics as leadership and vision, character and ethics, and gender and ethnicity. These are the essential elements in the development of self. Each president or leader must also learn to apply these petri dish ingredients to developing working relationships with others—the subject of Part Two of the book. Key groups include boards, sources of revenue, and the media.

These are not only important chapters but also highly informative ones. Carl Rogers taught us that we are all becoming. One does not wake up and "is" an effective president. Developing the fit between the individual and the organization is a function of what the person brings to the job and what the content of the job brings to the person. New leaders come to the presidency with motivation and expectations and bring within themselves energy and the potential to perform effectively. The keys to their successful performance are in organizing work in such a way as to meet this vision and to align that vision with the needs of their followers. Part Three of this book provides great wisdom into the tasks inherent in this extremely important symbiotic relationship.

The essays by other presidents that appear in this book are important contributions. They reinforce the concepts presented by Cathryn but also present unique experiences and personalities. I sincerely believe that you will enjoy this book and will be enriched through the first-person accounts of very exceptional and unique leaders.

George A. Baker III
Joseph D. Moore Distinguished Professor of Community College Leadership
North Carolina State University
Raleigh, NC
August, 1994

ACKNOWLEDGMENTS

Undertaking a project such as this one is never easy and gets completed because of the support of a wide variety of people. My thanks go to the Berkshire Community College Board of Trustees for granting me some time to work on the project in the face of uninformed and undeserved criticism of that decision; my thanks to those who chose to participate in this endeavor by spending time writing down their thoughts about the community college presidency; thanks to the President's Academy of AACC and all that I learned from my colleagues; and thanks to my personal friends who read the manuscript, critiqued it honestly, and assured me that they were not bored by it all. Finally, this book is for the man at the gas station in West Stockbridge, Massachusetts, who, when he read in the local paper that I was writing a book, admonished me "not to forget the little guys." I hope that I haven't.

PREFACE

Some people plan to become college presidents and succeed in achieving that goal; some people plan to become presidents but don't achieve that goal; and some people never plan to become presidents but get there anyway because of the circumstances in which they find themselves. Whatever the case, the presidency, once achieved, will never be what was expected simply because there are few ways in which to describe the job and few ways in which to explain how a presidency "feels." Presidents therefore usually write and talk about the technical side of the job and how we spend time. More challenging, however, is to convey the dramatic as well as the subtle changes that occur in how you are treated, how you are perceived, and how you are constantly evaluated against that background of the symbol(s) you represent to the institution.

The following chapters and individual essays are designed to explore not only what others say about issues and emotions relevant to the presidency, but also to convey in personal terms what the presidency means to those of us who are there now. Others who wish to follow these steps will, we hope, be better prepared, while those who are merely curious about community college presidents will better understand.

1

Making Choices

I have to confess: for a long time it never occurred to me to aspire to the position of community college president. In fact, wanting to be a college president didn't occur to me until well into my career as a teacher and student services administrator. I also must confess that to this day, I have not yet met that person who clearly articulated at an early age that his or her goal in life was to become a community college president.

WHY ARE WE HERE?

The most apparent question, then, is where do we all come from? How is it that this confederacy of over 1,000 souls nationwide either barely planned entrance into the presidency or got there even more incidentally? In the spring and summer of 1992 I asked about one hundred of my colleagues what led them down this path; some interesting answers were peppered throughout the expected ones:

> I wanted to try out my vision of what an effective community college should be.

> I wanted to prove I could perform at that level.

> It's the top position, something I have always aspired to since entering the ranks of the community college.

> I became a college president to reach my full potential as an educator and to better provide for my family.

> To put my educational philosophy into action, providing access to higher education for those who would normally not take advantage of the opportunities a post-secondary education offers.

To exert influence in a broader arena.

Former community college student, commitment to mission, luck.

I applied for the presidency after having the opportunity to serve as Acting President. I never intended or wanted to be a president. I found it 'fit' better than I had imagined.

On a psycho-social level, I became a college president out of a crazy notion that I could make a difference where others I observed were not even trying… On a personal level I became a college president because I had a need to answer an inner calling to do more than I was.

I became a college president because I wanted to do so and knew I could. If I had been a male, I would be leading a Fortune 500 firm.

By far the most common response to the question was that these individuals wanted to make a difference and believed that they could do so. Since relatively few of them said that the community college presidency had been a specific goal, one could draw the conclusion that those who want to lead, to control, to influence, to "make a difference" will manage to do that no matter where they find themselves.

There is, though, one other possibility that may support a positive stereotype about community college presidents: with very few exceptions, we are obsessively committed to a shared concept about community colleges being an indispensable part of higher education in this country. We can all go on endlessly about the value of "America's Colleges" and how we have helped transform the social landscape in this country. Sometimes others must wonder if our zealotry is born of a sense of inferiority; or if the relative newness of community colleges still makes us want to boast, like the nouveau riche; or if we feel that we have to continually justify our existence in the essentially medieval yet well accepted and understood world of the university. Or perhaps it is just that community college presidents spend so much time being the cheerleaders for our institutions that we perform at a moment's notice. All of us have that next Rotary speech composed before the invitation to speak is even in the mail.

WHERE DO WE COME FROM?

A study done by Clark Kerr and Marian Gade in 1986 entitled *The Many Lives of Academic Presidents* states that eighty-five percent of all presidents have had previous academic and administrative experience and that most also come from the same general type of institution of which they become a president (eighty percent of community college presidents came from community college ranks, for example). However, as we anticipate what the future holds for community colleges and for our social order, we must also be realistic about the kinds of leaders who will be the most effective for us.

The "conventional wisdom" has been that effective presidents must come from the academic ranks— must have been teachers at some point in their careers, become academic administrators, and risen to at least the academic dean level. During the various recessionary years when funding, or the lack thereof, was paramount it was occasionally possible to become a president by moving through the financial ranks. The person who had experience in business or finance, preferably in a community college setting was ahead of the competition, and experience managing the financial side of a college was seen as providing leadership experience necessary for a president. Concurrently, the person rising through the ranks within the student services segment of the community college was generally given less attention and seen as less of a presidential caliber leader. Even though we have prided ourselves on being student-centered institutions, there has been an underlying caste system within a college which suggests that issues related to student life outside the classroom are secondary and that therefore, leaders in that area are also secondary.

Years ago when my mentors encouraged me to consider aspiring to a presidency, they also unanimously told me that I would never get there if I didn't get out of the student services area and back over to academic affairs. I dare say I was not the only one getting that kind of advice and that what they were telling me was indeed true at that time (Vaughan, 1987).

In addition, there were also issues of race and gender. It was even more important for women and minorities to be seen as being strong academic leaders, and the woman or minority with financial experience or expertise was a treasure almost beyond recognition.

While the above statements are somewhat simplistic, it still is true that there are some assumptions about who is or who is not qualified to be a community college president which may no longer be accurate—even though those assumptions served us well in the past. We have moved into a new era with new expectations of our presidents. Not only must they have valid experiences which prepare them for a community college presidency, but they also must satisfy other institutional values: diversity, inclusiveness, opportunity for all, vision. The presidents of the future must be ready to become symbols and to be judged by the symbolic as well as by any accomplishments.

INTERNAL VS. EXTERNAL CANDIDACY

Assuming that the vast majority of community college presidents reach the position from somewhere within the community college system, two obvious paths emerge: one path takes an individual from the same college and over the years that path leads most likely from faculty member to division or department chair to dean or vice-president to president. It is also not uncommon for a person who came in to an institution as a dean or vice-president to eventually become the president of that institution. This internal path may take ten to twenty years and probably will occur in an institution which is relatively stable in all other respects. And the individual traveling that path must be successful in all positions he or she has held. The single institution presidency, as it will be called, is probably less common in community college careers than in other segments of higher education, but it certainly is not rare.

While many first generation presidents came from other segments of higher education and/or government, by the second generation of presidents the vast majority came from a community college background (Vaughan, 1986). The same is holding true for those of us in this third generation, and evidence of the single institution president is increasing. There is an enormous strain on an institution as it searches for a new president, especially on the smaller institutions with fewer resources, both human and financial. Thus, opportunities for those who have worked at one college for much if not all of their careers are still open. In addition, as the community college has embraced diversity and collegiality in its mission, many colleges look to previously ignored internal candidates for leadership, especially if those internal candidates are minority or female.

Nonetheless, the most common manner in which individuals reach the presidency is by coming in from another institution. Again according to Kerr and Gade, that number has been as high as eighty percent. Many boards will still opt for the external person if there is a perceived need for some kind of fundamental change at the institution, and if no internal candidates emerge as the type of leader who can bring about that change. It is a widely held belief as well that "the expert is the one who lives somewhere else" and that only by searching outside of the institution can a true savior be found. Or, if there is more than one internal or local candidate, boards will often desire to avoid the conflict that may arise or the political pressure that will be brought to bear and choose from the beginning to eliminate any consideration of internal candidates. More important, however, than analyzing why some internal candidates get considered and others don't is the effect on the president who eventually is selected—either internally or externally.

Daniel Moore, President of Haywood Community College in North Carolina, has had the experience both ways. His first presidency was at the institution where he had been a dean for eight years, and his second presidency has been at an institution where he came in from another state. He observes that there are indeed differences in the two experiences. Becoming the president where he had been a dean meant that his working relationships changed but had to change within the context of friendships already developed and ties already established on a social level. While he found this difficult, it did work and was not impossible. However, it should be a consideration for someone contemplating the possibility of becoming a president within his or her home institution. One must be honest about both working and social relationships and know from the beginning that changes will occur.

The possibility of applying for but not being selected for the presidency of one's institution must also be considered. There are definitely prices to be paid on both sides of the equation. An internal applicant has to be prepared for the decision to be made if the bid is unsuccessful: will you be able to stay in your present position and work for someone else? If not, are you prepared to apply for other jobs and to leave the institution which has been your home for (usually) a very long time?

Yet another issue which must be considered could be defined as self esteem. Since most presidential searches involve the entire college community in one way or another, the unsuccessful internal candidate must be ready to deal with the reality of not having been selected by those with whom he or she has worked. As rational as one is about it, the emotions surrounding rejection can be strong indeed. All of us can rationalize rejection by strangers ("If they don't want me, then that is not the place I wanted to work anyway"), but rejection by our friends and colleagues is much more difficult.

Finally, the stress of the search itself is evident and potentially more disturbing for the internal candidate. Without doubt there will be well intentioned friends and colleagues who offer support in the form of sharing the rumors which are rampant in a search process. Usually it is better **not** to know the details of a search, but the internal candidate may be subjected to more "support" than is usually needed, wanted or useful.

On the positive side, being selected for the presidency as an internal candidate has its advantages, not the least of which is that the process of discovery is lessened considerably. When one is already familiar with the institution and with the issues both on and underneath the surface, the amount of time spent getting to know people and their individual agendas is more productively spent on other concerns. The job itself is hard enough to get used to without the added disadvantage of not knowing where the skeletons are buried. At least a single institution president will know which ones can stay buried and which ones need to be exhumed.

Another advantage that has become more important to more people is

that the disruptions caused by having to physically move to another location are obviously not there. This is a factor which has changed many attitudes about career advancement at any cost, or the corporate model which,
even as adapted in education, has meant that one's bags had to be packed
at all times in order to work through the hierarchies with the hope of becoming a president. More women with family commitments have become
viable presidential candidates and there are more men who are viable presidential candidates who are married to women with careers. Thus, waiting
for opportunities at one's institution is becoming a more attractive alternative. It may no longer be true that the "place-bound" professional must
give up opportunities for advancement. Instead, any pressure in the future
to take advantage of local talent may result in increasing numbers of single
institution presidents, especially in the smaller community colleges or in
those with fewer resources and/or problems.

The other side of this issue is to look for a moment at the nature of the
president who comes to a college from somewhere else, which is the experience of still a majority of presidents, according to The American Council
on Education (1993). We have to spend more time and energy getting to
know people, the college and the community. We often have to move families and get children settled and figure out where to live. We have to develop working and social relationships and say "yes" to every invitation
until we have a better sense of what we can safely defer or decline. While
many first and second generation presidents may have had the luxury of
experimenting with the profession because there were so many opportunities available, that is no longer true for those of us in this generation, or
beyond. Even in 1981 when I chaired a presidential search committee for a
small, rural community college, we had almost two hundred applications,
mostly from inexperienced and unqualified people. While I didn't understand then what possessed so many glaringly inept candidates to apply for
a community college presidency, it is now no longer true that more applications come from unqualified and inexperienced persons than come from
those with solid backgrounds and strong commitments to the community
college. There are fewer presidencies available yet more people with potential to fill the position.

Regardless of one's circumstances, the point is that choosing to become a community college president must at some point be just that: a
choice. It is too important to everyone concerned not to make it a conscious
decision. Once the decision to become a president has been made, however, then no amount of energy spent in actively seeking the position or in
gaining experience is wasted. Even experiences which may seem negative
at the time can offer opportunities for learning.

CHOOSING TO LEAVE THE PRESIDENCY

Finally, if the choice to become a president must be a conscious one, as just asserted, then the choice about how long one remains in the job must also be a conscious one. Most presidents are hard workers, are used to succeeding, and for many, becoming a president represents the culmination of a career and the accomplishment of a valued goal.

Robert Birnbaum (1992) states it well: "College presidents are not immune from American values that prize accomplishment and view positions achieved through competence, dedication, and hard work as prizes, well earned and worth protecting." (p.194) However, it is also through his research that he has concluded that only one quarter of presidents will be "exemplary," while one half will be average and the last quarter unsuccessful. He also maintains that we still don't know enough about leadership to dramatically increase those who will be exemplary. Therefore, we should pay more attention to those who are average to try to increase their effectiveness and to keep them from falling into the bottom quarter of presidents deemed unsuccessful. One way of doing this is to make sure that there are honest appraisals of performance and honorable ways to leave an institution before it is too late.

None of us in the job want to think of ourselves as ever being in a negative situation, and no one who is aspiring to the position anticipates being anything but exemplary. The reality is, however, that to be an effective president one must not only work on developing the skills and attributes already discussed, but one must also be ready to accept that the presidency is not a sinecure. This is a job in which there is a lot of change and turnover, and one must make the decision going in that there will be a time when it is best to move on. Birnbaum concluded that there is "nothing inherently beneficial about long presidential terms, and on average, institutions might be better off with shorter rather than longer presidential tenures." (p.195) He also states that presidents "provide the greatest benefit to their colleges at two points in their careers: when they arrive, and when they leave." All of us want the leave-taking to be a personal decision, however, and one that is ultimately a positive one.

Vaughan (1989) says that there are signals one can notice to indicate that something is not working anymore. Some of those signals include developing too much routine, losing patience with constituents, feeling that nothing is exciting or having difficulty establishing priorities, noticing that *all* the grass starts looking greener, or simply acknowledging that the time has come or the agenda has been completed.

Or, one might get into the position and realize that it simply isn't what was expected and just isn't personally satisfying enough to put up with the perceived constraints. The point is that it is better to leave an unsatis-fying situation than it is to hang on for the wrong reasons. After all, most of us have changed jobs enough times over the years to know what is right for us and what isn't. It is just harder to "give up" on being a president because of the personal investment in success or achievement. Just as an institution judges a president for his or her symbolic value, we must be honest about the symbolic value we as individuals place on being a presi-dent. It is critical that we take the job seriously, but it is equally critical that we not get carried away with our own importance.

Most presidents with whom I have talked, however, have a pretty good sense of their situations. We go through cycles, too: the energetic, almost manic new president, all shiny and squeaky clean and ready to change the world; to the calmer and more realistic president who has experienced some success but has also felt the sting of erring; to the philosophical and some-what more emotionally detached president who is beyond being surprised by *anything*. One can be effective no matter what the cycle as long as the commitment to education is still alive, and the joy of learning is still para-mount. But when the joy is gone, it is time to search for it elsewhere rather than to burden an institution with a dispirited or indifferent leader. Our institutions deserve—and must have—better in order to thrive.

After Leaving, What?

Even if still happy in the position, presidents need to think about what comes after—what kind of professional fulfillment is possible if one is ready to leave the presidency but not ready to leave the profession. While Vaughan has surveyed presidents and written about "life after the presidency," nei-ther he nor anyone he has surveyed has any definite answers or "typical" patterns for community college presidents. Common choices include con-sulting or teaching. A few make a successful transition into corporate life, some try politics, and many simply retire.

Our career planning seems to stop with the presidency; we have not viewed the position as another step in a continuum. Thus, when a presi-dent finds out that the job is not a good fit, or when a president is told that it is time to move on, many are left bewildered because they have not planned beyond the presidency. Perhaps that is also why Birnbaum et al. find only a quarter of presidents to be exemplary: too many who are ill suited to the position stay because they don't know what else to do and haven't planned for another career shift.

The President's Academy of the American Association of Community Colleges has had some discussions concerning this career choice issue for presidents but is still in the elementary planning stages of providing any advice, information, or structures which may be used. Most community college presidents do not have academic rank or tenure as do our university colleagues. Thus, there really is no safety net within the educational profession, and we are very much on our own when critical junctions are reached.

Therefore, the third important component to consider when choosing to become a community college president is making sure there is a mechanism for moving on when the time is right. Otherwise, the alternative is to feel trapped or resentful or simply disengaged, which is hard on the individual but equally hard on the college. Think about it: if the average tenure of a college president is between five and seven years, and the average age for entering the presidency is in one's forties, then what happens to those productive years which we all still have prior to the average retirement at age 65? In their study done in 1986, Kerr and Gade noted that after the average seven year presidential stay, 15% move on to another presidency, 20% go back to faculty, 15% enter other administrative positions within higher education, 25% retire, and 25% leave academe all together. What isn't noted is the percentage of those who actually planned their next move and therefore maintained a modicum of control over their lives. It is time that we start to care as much about our own career decision-making process as we care about the decisions of our students or our children.

Essay

THE MOVING PRESIDENT: CHANGING INSTITUTIONS
by Ruth M. Smith

In the summer of 1991, we moved from the coalfields of southwestern Virginia to the cornfields of northwestern Illinois. It was a major move for my husband and me. We had made many personal and professional friends during my tenure as president of Mountain Empire Community College, and it was not easy to say farewell. But I was going to Highland Community College which was located in a city only 45 miles from my hometown and my husband, having grown up on a farm, was looking forward to watching the corn grow knee-high by the 4th of July.

The decision to change colleges is not an easy one. There are many complex factors to be considered, and they vary from person to person. It may be a desire to work in a different type of governance system or a different size institution. It may relate to geography, finances, or personal needs. It may be based upon the fact that the president and the college are no longer a fit. All of these are legitimate factors which must be weighed very carefully. The key to a successful move, regardless of the factors, is to make certain that one is moving toward a positive challenge rather than running away from something.

When moving toward a new opportunity, one needs to carefully assess whether or not she has the skills and attributes necessary to provide leadership in the new setting. One must clearly identify those ingredients which attract and believe that he or she can bring about positive change.

In my case, I was able to list several factors that were important to me. I was moving to a locally governed community college with some of the funding derived from local property taxes. Also, I was moving to a setting where there were more opportunities for students interested in athletics and the arts. In addition, the new college had some specific needs which my skills could address. These included fundraising and foundation experience, occupational program development skills, and an inclusive management style aimed at empowering employees to be both responsible and innovative. Finally, I was moving home to my "roots," and this was the driving personal motivator for me.

Saying "good-bye" was difficult. The final rush of farewell parties coupled with packing and preparing a house for sale took a great deal of energy. There were many tears over the last few days. In addition, there was the stress of completing tasks at MECC while thinking about the challenges coming at HCC. As one door was closing, another was opening, and the secret of success was in the timing. It was a process of letting go and taking hold at the same time. Emotions pulled in many directions, and I did my best to pay attention to those feelings and to deal with them forthrightly.

Driving from Virginia to Illinois was extremely important in making this transition. As we left the mountains, I felt a great sense of sadness. I remembered the uniqueness of my Appalachian friends, their strength and their creativity. The next day we entered the farmlands of Illinois. We felt a surge of excitement as we gazed at the tall stalks of corn. Both of us recalled our childhoods, farm chores, and the taste of milk fresh from the cow. Then we began to anticipate life in this familiar setting and feelings of joy began to emerge.

Soon we were in our new home unpacking the many boxes and wondering how we had managed to accumulate so many things. I had planned to have a few days for getting settled before my official duties began, but the evening of the day we moved into the house found us attending a small dinner party in our new community. Immediately I shifted gears from finding a new doctor and dentist to thinking about college issues. And thus I began the process of taking hold.

As an "experienced" president in a new setting, I soon found that there are both positives and negatives attached. Experience, if one has learned from it, increases confidence. In addition, it helps one to know how to approach new problems and situations. Finally, I believe that experience humbles us and helps us to put things in better perspective. This includes never taking yourself too seriously and learning how to laugh at yourself occasionally.

On the other hand, experience can cause problems. There is a tendency to want to recreate the positive aspects from the prior institution and to try to find people with the exact set of skills that were available before. It is important for the transplanted president to take time to study problems, gather information, and assess the talents of the current employees and faculty.

At times I have had a feeling of *déja vu* when a problem from MECC would reappear at HCC. We had spent a great deal of time and energy in Virginia developing assessment plans. Soon I found that we needed to do the same in Illinois. In that case, I was able to speak confidently about how to approach the task and why it was worth the effort.

In another case, a member of the student government asked if they could recommend new colors for the college. Having been through an attempt to do this at MECC, I was able to advise the student that this was emotional issue and to be careful to give faculty and staff an opportunity to voice their opinions.

A new president, with prior presidential experience, must explore many ways of obtaining information. One cannot know the strengths and weaknesses of a college simply through reading reports. I made it a priority to wander around the campus on a daily basis and to talk with faculty, staff and students in formal and informal settings. Not only did I learn a great deal from these meanderings, but I also quickly became attached to these "new" people in my life. It helped me to continue my process of letting go even though I was still calling my colleagues in Virginia on a weekly sometimes daily, basis.

After a few weeks, I was able to identify several initiatives which needed to begin immediately. One of these was the development of a strategic plan. This project quickly brought together the college community and representatives from many towns in our district. It was a positive experience and helped to bring about change by involving many people in planning our future.

While working to understand the college and its people, the "moving" president must also learn about the communities the college serves. Again, experience both facilitates and impedes. Often the political systems are different and must be learned. Sometimes the persons with the "important" titles are not the "movers and shakers" of the area. So, some energy must be saved for these important tasks.

There were days when I wondered how many more people I could greet with a smile, how many new challenges I could tackle, how many more nights my spouse would understand why I was not home, and how many more meetings I could attend. I occasionally wondered why I had ever decided it was time to move! Letting go and taking hold at the same time is not easy, and one must develop strategies for survival.

Looking back, there are many things I could have done that would have made the change smoother. On the other hand, I did do some things right. Most importantly, I said my "good-byes" with care. I made certain that I had some alone time with special people. In some cases, I declined invitations to one last dinner party in order to save time for those people who were most important to me.

Most importantly, I did what was best for my family. I managed to find a new home which we could occupy immediately before I started my new responsibilities. This was important because my spouse wanted to join me immediately and because I knew myself well enough to know that I needed to have my house in some semblance of order before I began my work. And, I knew that once my job began, I would have no time for arranging my home. What is "right" will vary from family to family. The key is to know what right is and then to do it.

In reflecting on what it is like to move from one presidency to another, I can best sum it up by quoting Charles Dickens who once wrote: "It was the best of times and the worst of times." For me, it was a mix of sadness in leaving and joy in arriving, confidence from experience with anxiety about the challenges of a new setting, the stress of moving with the rush of energy that comes with meeting new people and setting new goals, loyalty to the former institution with visions held for the new college.

Myriad competing emotions had to be examined, felt, and properly utilized for forward movement. Having done it, I would not recommend it to the weak of heart. It takes tenacity and belief in yourself and in the future of both institutions. Most of all, it means being able to let go and take hold at the same time. Therein lies the challenge and the reward.

Occasionally when I gaze at the rolling cornfields through my kitchen window, I see the beautiful mountains of southwestern Virginia. Then I wonder how they are doing and hope that all goes well. One must let go, but one can never forget.

Ruth M. Smith is President of Highland Community College in Freeport, IL. She has served as a representative from the central region to the American Association of Community Colleges' President's Academy Executive Committee and on the AACC Board of Directors.

Part I

DEVELOPING OURSELVES

The topics next discussed may be the topics most analyzed when people talk and write about presidents or CEOs, but that does not mean that they are the ones best understood. Leadership can be learned and developed, vision comes with experience, character is probably formed by the time we start to walk and talk as infants, and ethics represent standards of behavior which are assimilated from our cultural teachings. All of these elements help form our personalities, just as our experiences help form our attitudes. The goal of all of us, whether we are presidents or observers of presidents, is somehow to make sense of the job by trying to establish the standards in each category by which we can measure ourselves and others. In other words, the more abstract the concept, the more we try to make it concrete through definition and evaluation. This is a crazy business.

2

Leadership and Vision

LEADERSHIP

Much has been written about leadership in the past thirty or so years, ranging from Fielder's contingency theory to McClelland's expectancy theory to Hersey and Blanchard's situational leadership theory. Numerous tests have been designed to measure leadership qualities and general management style, such as the Leadership Behavior Description Questionnaire or Blake and Mouton's Managerial Grid. All agree that leadership is a function of one's position, behavior, personality, or the situation and cannot be defined only by traits or behaviors. And even though most leadership theories focus on more than one dimension, they still can be categorized under two general concepts: goal achievement and group maintenance. In other words, leaders are measured and defined by how well they as individuals are able to accomplish goals that have been outlined by the group being led, and then by their ability to keep the group working together to achieve those goals. Thus, leaders must exhibit concern for organizational tasks and concern for individual relationships in order to be considered effective. Sounding so simple in theory belies the reality of defining leadership on which so many prominent thinkers have spent so much time.

LEADERSHIP VS. MANAGEMENT

Perhaps the difficulty is not in defining leadership but in defining *effective* leadership. Words such as "visionary" or "pathfinder" are often used to describe effective leaders, and writers such as Argyris and Cyert (1980) go to great lengths to distinguish leadership from management, including statements that effective management is possible even without effective leadership. Again, the research boils down to one pervasive conclusion: it depends on the situation. What makes a leader effective in one organization might doom that same leader to ignominy in another.

As presidents, we like to think of ourselves as leaders rather than managers. The connotations of "leadership" are much loftier than the pedestrian associations that go with "management," especially in the academic setting. As Madeleine Green states in *Leaders for a New Era* (1988, p. 16), "The true member of the academic community is expected to long for the classroom and the library. Management connotes the mundane, the operational, the ability to get things done toward the accomplishment of a predetermined goal. Leadership, on the other hand, provides shape, direction, and meaning, and is therefore far more intellectually respectable."

Argyris and Cyert define management as "the art of allocating resources within the organization in a manner designed to reach the goals of the organization" and leadership as " the art of stimulating the human resources within the organization to concentrate on total organizational goals rather than on individual subgroup goals." (p. 63) In spite of our preference of leadership over management, when we are being honest, we will admit that leadership is but one function of the president's position, and that much of the rest of what we do is manage.

Eras of Management and Leadership

In his book, *A Briefing For Leaders*, Robert Dilenschneider (1992) discusses power, leadership, and communications. He also says that there indeed is a difference between leadership and management, but that there is another distinct concept, administration, which helps to form the three distinct eras he outlines.

First, he maintains that in the 1950s and 1960s there was power as administration, with the "watchwords" being conformity and order. However, power as administration ended when computers started taking over routine tasks, decision-making became more decentralized and a new weight was given to interpersonal skills.

His second point is that the 1970s and 1980s were the era of power by management, where managers learned that "they could exert power by initiating fundamental changes in their organizations." (p. 4) He concludes this particular discussion by asserting that in the 1990s we are entering the era of leadership as power because of the enormous changes and instability in the world. There is a yearning for something beyond management, which too often led the manager to act out of self interest and therefore to manipulate rather than to lead. His opinion is best stated in the following excerpt:

> Leadership has become the important 'value added' for being on top
> in the nineties. When power was management, managers hunted down

exceptions. If they were bad, they were ruthlessly eliminated. If they were good, they became a new performance standard. Today, the leader is focused neither on securing order nor on rooting out exceptions but on providing a vision. (p. 6)

Leadership and Power

In 1984, the Commission on Presidential Leadership concluded that the previous twenty years produced a measurable weakening of the presidency in higher education which in turn has weakened higher education itself. Therefore, as stated by the Commission, "... strengthening presidential leadership is one of the most urgent concerns on the agenda of higher education in the United States (p. 102)." But what does that mean? Since 1984 both internal and external constraints have increased, hampering presidents from exercising leadership as it is traditionally understood: there is more competition for students, even among community colleges; the costs of operating have grown almost exponentially in comparison to the dramatic decreases in public funding; there is a decided lack of trust and confidence in public education at all levels; and employment agreements have become highly formalized, leading to the increasing presence of a labor/management mentality on many campuses. If strengthening presidential leadership means doing away with the constraints of competition for students, or releasing us from the stranglehold of not having adequate resources from year to year, or reestablishing a level of trust both within and outside the institution, then it may be possible and the Commission may be right.

It is ultimately impossible to talk about leadership without talking about power, however, even though the two terms are not synonymous. We must recognize that in the 1990s community college presidents may de facto have less power within the institution than at any other time in our brief history, partially because of the factors just mentioned. Yet it never has been true in higher education that a president exercises "leadership" by making decisions and then having others carry them out, which would be a traditional way to think about "power." There has always been a system of checks and balances, starting with faculty, which has precluded the president from acting autonomously, even though we might like to on many occasions. The governance systems of most colleges are really quite complex, including elements such as curriculum committees which control academic course and program offerings, or different forms of faculty senates which often want to control just about everything else. Presidential decision-making and autonomy are almost oxymorons in this age of collegiality and collective bargaining. The mistaken belief that the position of president equals unlimited power in the institution has led to many bad decisions and many unpopular presidents.

Nonetheless, if a president is to exhibit true leadership, which can influence the amount of power the president is perceived to have, it may mean behaving in a way within the institution which eventually changes the reward systems by creating a climate for risk taking and for innovation, as opposed to a climate valuing the status quo. It may also mean forcing oneself, as well as the institution, to get to, or stay on, the cutting edge of the technological revolution, all the while establishing processes and an atmosphere which will promote the integration of new technology into the mission and core values of the institution. It may mean taking planning seriously and committing human and financial resources to the building of arks rather than to the predicting of the rain.

New Dimensions of Leadership

In that our institutions are all strapped for resources, our students are in greater need of financial help to meet college costs, and our communities have unmet needs which are staggering, how we demonstrate leadership as community college presidents may have to take on new dimensions as well. It may also have to be demonstrated outside the institution in addition to inside. For all of us who still "want to make a difference," let's look at where that might be:

Organizational Development. Our colleges have now labored for decades with fairly "traditional" organizational structures: there are academic departments administered by department chairs or division chairs or assistant deans; there are professionals who are lumped into the categories of student services who, although dealing with the same students as the academic folks, often have little communication or interaction with faculty or academic administrators on a regular basis—unless it is to respond to some sort of problem. It might be time for presidents, who are still educators, to lead the challenge to academic tradition by getting other educators (faculty and staff) to discuss the possibility that there might be other and better ways we can serve our students. Colleges that have pioneered new ways of organizing academically (into learning clusters or learning communities instead of subject matter-based departments, for example), have experienced great success with their students. More presidents who participate in the academic life of the college need to ask the hard questions and force faculty to question the assumptions on which they have always operated. True leadership for the future may lie in doing whatever it takes to counteract willingness to accept the academic status quo.

Resource Development. A president in these times who is not spending time hustling money for the institution is rare. For those of us who are funded publicly, our time is spent convincing local legislators that our community college is and must remain a budgetary priority. We inform, we argue, we cajole, we plead, we brag about our institution's good deeds. We do anything we can think of to convince the public that their tax dollars are being well spent. We also have established non-profit foundations which are becoming increasingly important to us as public funding sources evaporate. The president is the one who must make the foundation profitable so that the institution will benefit. Finally, we have become, in many small communities, the embodiment of higher education — its virtues as well as its faults. A presidential priority has become community visibility, and any president who is not out there is, in the opinion of many, not demonstrating the fiscal leadership that is needed today.

Student Resources. Closely related to resource development is the president's role in helping identify the resources students need to help them pay our costs. Raising scholarship dollars is easier than convincing governments to allocate dollars to an institution, and yet it is something that I think we presidents don't do as well—or as frequently—as we could. We are all watching our private college counterparts and adopting from them their successful techniques: strong and devoted alumni associations, foundations focused on fund raising and providing access to individuals with money to donate, increased allocations of internal funds for scholarship or work study aid. In addition, however, we must continue providing leadership for things community colleges have developed to a greater extent than other segments of higher education: provisions for child care, academic calendars and schedules which accommodate working and part-time students, accessibility of locations, and wider acceptance of institutional austerity in order to keep costs down.

Community Needs. Rhetoric to the contrary notwithstanding, this country has been in a recession for some time. The future is more uncertain for many than it has ever been. Our communities have desperate needs: roads need to be paved, health care costs cannot be allowed to consume entire municipal budgets, and civil liberties must be protected in the face of increasing incidents of sociopathic behavior. Finally, citizens must be educated and trained to fill whatever jobs are left, or created in the future. Obviously the community college president cannot single-handedly solve these community problems, but we must make sure that we are involved in whatever solutions are being tried in our communities. For example, this may mean demonstrating leadership by campaigning for funding for K-12 education, or being visibly active in community efforts to curb substance abuse and its attendant consequences, or speaking out for community development issues which will lead to positive economic growth. These issues have everything to do with the quality of education we can offer at the community college and the president is the one who must work hard for the community. One way of looking at it is that all residents of our service area are students of the college whether or not they are actually "enrolled."

Leadership, then, is possible in the future, but it may not resemble the leadership of the past. In many ways, leadership of a community college is becoming more abstract. Not only have the topics requiring presidential leadership changed but also the environment in which leadership can occur has narrowed over the years. It is most ironic that in many ways a president may have more influence outside an institution than inside. That is what is meant by abstract leadership: it is becoming more removed from the traditional measures to determine effectiveness, such as number of buildings built or number of programs added to the curriculum. Instead, effectiveness is measured by how well we represent the institution to the community, how well we can articulate institutional goals to the politicians and media, and how we are "perceived" by the various constituencies. Leaders are still concerned with helping the institution meet its goals and with maintaining the spirit of the groups working there, but the paradigm may have shifted to the world outside the institution.

Reconciling Leadership and Management

Even though the concept of management has often been separated from leadership, as mentioned earlier, it cannot be ignored as an important component which is related to how a president is perceived as a leader. Indeed, the language used to talk about life in organizations is full of references to managing: managing change, managing finances, managing enrollment, managing quality, managing human resources, managing time. If one can't manage, how is one supposed to lead? The dilemma for community college presidents is not unlike the dilemma for corporate executives: managing the daily life of the organization leaves little time to lead. But if one doesn't lead, then trying to manage the organization ultimately is meaningless — either it will cease to exist, or it will have found a "leader" somewhere else.

Perhaps, then, the reconciliation of leadership and management is as follows: to be a leader, one must be able to manage in such a way that the ordinary coexists with the extraordinary. For example, almost every higher education institution in this country is presently engaged in, has been engaged in, or has at least talked "total quality management." Awhile back, it was management by objectives. Then came "re-engineering" management theory. Whatever it is called, more attention is being paid to the management of organizations, and the president is called upon to devote more time and energy "leading" the institution down the newest path to Oz. It has been proven repeatedly that without presidential commitment and "leadership", TQM does not work. Or MBO doesn't work. Or XYZ doesn't work. Thus, the president must behave as a manager dealing with the ordinary functions of the organization while thinking as a leader, always on the alert for a more effective way to "manage" and willing to risk the difficulty of change in order to take advantage of the extraordinary opportunities which the future holds. Perhaps the real link between management and leadership is vision.

VISION

Vision, a concept that is closely intertwined with leadership these days, is no easier to define or identify. In their 1989 book entitled *Shared Vision: Transformational Leadership in American Community Colleges,* Roueche, Baker and Rose define leadership as it applies to the community college: "Leadership is the ability to influence, shape, and embed values, attitudes, beliefs, and behaviors consistent with increased staff and faculty commitment to the unique mission of the community college." (p.18) As they reached for a better way of talking about the type of leadership that transforms an institution and which everyone become more than they believed was possible, the authors turn to a lengthy discussion of the role that "vision" plays in effective leadership:

> All the writers on transformational leadership, however, identify one central theme that recurs in descriptions of transformational leaders—the role of vision. These researchers corroborate our findings by emphasizing that the powerful leaders of the past and present were dreamers and visionaries. These were people who looked beyond the confines of space and time to transcend the traditional boundaries of either their positions or their organizations. (p.109)

While most of us who are presidents have an inclination to look to the future and have a sense of where our institutions are (or should be) going, we may not be visionary. Having vision is not something one is born with, nor is it always possible to acquire vision through training. Rather, it may be the best combination of both a personality type and an accumulation of experience—the embodiment of nature and nurture. One who is a natural optimist, a risk taker, an improviser, or one who is challenged by adversity may one day be labeled a "visionary." However, the label won't be applied until that person has gained a wealth of experience and has failed as well as succeeded. Presidents studied by Roueche et al. who were considered "transformational leaders" and therefore by definition considered visionary were also those who had been presidents for a number of years. They had a great deal of knowledge about what was possible for community colleges as well as the benefit of having had the opportunity to flourish in environments conducive to growth and change.

Green states (1988) that the environment for leadership has so changed in the late 1980s and early 1990s that even though good management will always be vital, "campuses and society will look to academic leaders to clarify their institutional missions, to articulate an academic vision, and to be accountable for the quality of their programs and graduates. They will have to do all in an atmosphere of growing external controls, decreased institutional autonomy, and generally scarce resources." (p. 36) Vision as it applies to anything other than the academic arena, however, is not mentioned.

Tasks of Leadership and Vision

In 1986 John Gardner wrote about the nine tasks which are the "eternal functions of leadership": envisioning goals, affirming values, motivating, managing, achieving workable unity, explaining, serving as a symbol, representing the group, and renewing. Green would modify that list, emphasizing five tasks especially important to leaders in academe in the future: "serving as a symbol, achieving workable unity, serving as a team leader, as an information executive, and as a future agent." (p.38)

Her view is that we have moved to a post managerial era and that while the basic tasks of leaders do not change, the relative importance of those tasks does. The word vision is missing from her list, although in her discussion of the symbolic function of the leader, she does acknowledge that the president embodies the "communal educational vision." (p. 38) She concludes that the symbolic function of leadership, that which is perhaps the closest to the visionary function of a leader, is not only the most difficult of all the leadership tasks but is also the one that is the most likely to be learned by example and experience.

One of the most provocative new books on leadership and vision is *Leadership and the New Science* by Margaret Wheatley (1992). She conceives of organizational vision "as a field—a force of unseen connections that influences employees' behavior—rather than as an evocative message about some desired future state." (p.13) Using quantum physics and principles of the behavior of natural organisms and systems, Wheatley has come to a new understanding of organizations and what will help them be viable in the future. She states that we need to see organizations not as machines, a la Taylor, but rather as "process structures". Therefore, in her design, a "visionary leader" would be one who can build relationships, nurture growth and evolution, and understand that power is based on energy.

A contrasting point of view was presented by Richard Chait, professor of higher education and management at the University of Maryland. He wrote an article for *The Chronicle of Higher Education* (September 22, 1993) in which he decried the emphasis on vision for college presidents. He states that the desire for a president to be a visionary leader may be somewhat misplaced, and that the reality is that a president's vision "will be far more evident through a rear-view mirror when the incumbent leaves office…" He believes that presidents need to spend far more time and energy on the basics of providing institutional leadership and less time worrying about having a vision because the institution will go the direction it is headed usually in spite of presidential vision, not because of it. Chait believes that "the virtues of vision have been exaggerated…these are not the times for heady visions anyway, which typically entail new expenditures that seldom are offset by comparable reductions elsewhere in the organization. These are, instead, the times for sober calculations and pragmatic stratagems." (p. B2)

Even though we may not be able to conclusively define vision, or agree on its relative importance to effective leadership, it is one of those attributes that we all recognize. Remember President Bush and "the vision thing"? He was haunted by the media for his inability to articulate a vision for the country. As a result, he was perceived by many as a shallow thinker with no commitment to values of any kind. While it may not be as important for a community college president to be perceived as having vision as it obviously is for the President of the United States, the "vision thing" still remains a part of leadership that helps ultimately to define the quality of a presidency. But it is not something that we are born with. Rather, vision is an acquisition paid for by experience and reflection, and valued because it is rare.

The vision of President Truman to foresee a truly democratic approach to higher education that became the community college is not likely to be repeated any time soon. However, as community college presidents we can still work on honing our visions for our institutions and for our communities. Vision in the future will mean thinking proactively, taking advantage of even the smallest opportunity to educate people or do something to improve the quality of life, and maintaining a belief in the essential goodness in people regardless of growing evidence to the contrary. Our ability to be visionary leaders in the community college setting is going to be challenged by the growing number of events which dictate our circumstances and over which we have very little control. As best stated by Roueche, Baker, and Rose, the critical variable in successful visionary, or transformational leadership is the ability of the leader to have an impact on the behavior of the followers. Their transformational leaders "possess imagination and creativity that, when combined with their ability to interrelate with their organizations or institutions, provide a climate conducive to new beginnings." (p.289) If we have the energy to try to live up to that standard, even in the face of difficult circumstances, then perhaps we can all be visionary presidents.

3

Character and Ethics

CHARACTER

Another element which is critical to being an effective president is one of those hard to define attributes called character. One way of observing character is to examine how a person assumes the roles they are expected to play as president. One of the best descriptions of these roles comes from Henry Mintzberg in *The Nature of Managerial Work* (1973). He says that there are ten roles which are divided into three basic groups: interpersonal, informational, and decisional.

Interpersonal Roles

In the interpersonal category are the roles of *figurehead,* during which we perform routine duties of a legal or social nature. We attend openings, receptions, inaugurals, commencements, convocations, etc. and represent the institution as the figurehead. Most times these appearances are passive, but there are many in which we play an active role as a guest speaker or master of ceremonies.

The second interpersonal role is that of *leader,* which already has been discussed to some extent. In that role we become responsible for the motivation of subordinates, for staffing and training and certain types of decision-making, and for standard setting. The third interpersonal role is that of *liaison,* in which we develop and maintain a network of contacts who provide us with information, and at times with favors.

Informational Roles

The informational roles include *monitor* and *disseminator*. As monitors we seek and receive wide varieties of information in order to develop our understanding of the organization and the environment. Then we disseminate or transmit this information, some of which is factual and some of which has involved interpretation of differing positions, to other members of the organization. We then also play the information role of *spokesperson*, transmitting information to outsiders about the organization's plans or policies or actions.

Decisional Roles

The last general category identified by Mintzberg is the decisional category, which includes four roles. First is that of *entrepreneur,* searching organizations and the environment for opportunities or projects to bring about change. Another role is that of *disturbance handler*, taking responsibility for correcting disturbances or solving problems. Third is the role of *resource allocator*, the position of either making or approving all significant organizational decisions. Last is the role of *negotiator*, responsible for representing the organization at major negotiations, either with other organizations or with employment units such as faculty associations or collective bargaining units.

It is not uncommon in the experience of most presidents to have to fulfill most, if not all, of those roles in the course of a single day. That is what makes this job fascinating as well as exhausting. The concern here, though, is not necessarily to elaborate on each role but rather to make a general observation: as important as it is to keep track of which role we are playing in which situation, it is equally important not to lose track of who we are at the core. In other words, it is not possible to successfully fulfill others' expectations in various situations if we do not have a very strong sense of self to begin with. I have thought about this sense of self for many years—it is something I recognize when I see it and know also when it is missing. While the details have long since faded from my mind, I know that over the years I have worked for or known presidents who were very effective and some who were spectacularly ineffective. The major difference between them has not been in their intentions but rather in their overall approach to the roles they had to play. Presidents who have been effective have had, above all else, a strong core personality with which they were comfortable. That is what is meant by a sense of self; they have been able to transcend the roles and remain true to that strong core personality.

Stages of Leadership and Power

Another way of looking at this phenomenon of character is through a model of the stages of leadership and personal power developed by Hagberg (1983). Her model shows six stages of power:

Stage One really represents powerlessness, where one manipulates others and uses force to lead, inspiring fear in others to gain power. At this stage the person is dependent on getting things through others, has relatively low self-esteem, and often has little information or skill.

Stage Two is power by association, where one leads by seduction, makes deals, and inspires dependence among subordinates. Again, self-esteem is relatively low, and the person at this stage has a high need for security.

Stage Three exhibits power through symbols. The person in this stage leads by personal persuasion and inspires a winning attitude, but it really is a control stage. There are rules, rewards, and symbols of power, even though the person at this stage may have a great deal of charisma which attracts followers.

Stage Four is called power by reflection. The person at this stage is respected for his or her competence, strength of character, and ability to mentor. The person at this stage leads by modeling integrity and inspiring hope in others. It is a time of intense reflection and the emergence of what we have been calling leadership.

Stage Five may be the closest to describing what I have been calling a sense of self. Hagberg says that at this stage the person has vision, leads by empowering others, and inspires love and service. There is self acceptance at this stage, and a more diminished ego.

Stage Six is what she calls power by gestalt— the person leads by being wise and inspiring inner peace. The presidents whom I have known who have reached this stage have truly been the good ones and the ones I constantly hope we all emulate. As difficult as this job is from time to time, perhaps the most difficult part of it is focusing on this issue of character and remembering that the more we empower others, the more we get back. The more we can depend on our inner strength and personal integrity, the closer we can come to being true leaders.

ETHICS

Of all the undefinables for presidents, ethics is at the top of the list in spite of its casual treatment by Webster ("A principal of right or good behavior; the rules or standards of conduct governing the members of a profession.") A great deal of very productive time has been spent on this subject, notably by the AACC President's Academy under the leadership of Daniel F. Moriarty in 1989 and 1990. We now have published and widely agreed upon statements of Ethics for Boards and for Presidents which many presidents have used to foster additional discussions about institutional ethics on their campuses. It may be, however, that all that we have finally agreed upon is that the topic is important and needs to be discussed. We also agree that presidents in particular, since they in so many ways "represent" the institution, must be ethical. That is about as far as it goes— from here on we are on our own.

It is possible to see ethical questions in just about everything we do or in the decisions we are asked to make. The most obvious situations are never the troubling ones, either. We know what to do when confronted by glaring breaches of institutional codes of conduct, such as lying or cheating or stealing. The difficult decisions to handle ethically are those involving the more subtle shades of human behavior and differing interpretations of reality. There are also times when doing what is "right" is not always apparent just as there often are conflicts between what is best for the greatest number of people or for the institution as a whole, and what may be best for certain individuals. Making these kinds of choices does involve ethics, as fuzzy as that term might become in some situations. The president must have a very strong sense of what is fair, must be able to anticipate consequences of choices made, and must be able to focus on the problem at hand while everyone else is expressing opinions about what should or should not be done. When I first became a president I was asked in an interview how this job was different from others I had held now that there were hundreds of employees reporting to me rather than handfuls. My first answer, which to still accurate to this day, was that it simply meant there were that many more people who were anxious to tell me how to do the job.

Absolutely everyone has an opinion about how a president should behave and how the president should make decisions. But that is not a problem — sometimes an annoyance, perhaps, but not a problem. The difficulty is in dealing with the results of decisions, especially when the decisions may not be popular ones. It is then that those who disagree will start talking about ethics.

Questions to Ask and Answer

As we try to sort through the thornier issues with which one is faced as a president, there are several questions to ask oneself regardless of the specific issue. First, is absolutely all the information at hand that is needed in order to make a decision? Presidents find themselves in unnecessary binds when they must make choices based on incomplete pictures. Since there are usually fifteen sides to every story, even when only two people are involved, it is imperative that the president get as much information as possible before reaching any conclusions.

The next question involves legalities. Have any violations of law or of contract occurred? It is always nice to have something legal to hang your hat on if you want to avoid making a judgment. Usually, however, the issues are not that clearly laid out. Most of us do not break the law knowingly, and most contractual disputes are based on interpretation rather than on blatant disregard of the agreements outlined. The legal questions must still be asked, however, before moving on to the next questions, which are about fairness. Has everyone directly involved had an opportunity to present a point of view? Are there any compromises which will bring people together so that they can all live with the solution eventually reached? What might be the unintended consequences of this decision?

One specific true story here illustrates the above points. A dean came in to tell the president that he had just received a letter from a travel agency in New York City containing some rather alarming information. The president couldn't imagine what a travel agent in New York had to do with that college but listened intently to what the dean had learned. This travel agent alleged that one of the faculty members had represented herself to this agent as an official of the college in charge of travel programs and as such was making arrangements with this agent to provide her with business from the college in exchange for free airplane tickets for the faculty member. The president's internal alarms started going off immediately, knowing that a potential fraud situation was going to lead to some sort of confrontation with the faculty member, who was on sabbatical and unavailable for several weeks. The faculty member was eventually contacted so that the president could hear another side of the story which with luck would have less ominous overtones. Unfortunately, the allegations of the travel agent were admitted to by the faculty member, along with several other things, and at that point the president knew that life had just become immensely more complicated because of a decision that would have to be made. Looking at the legal aspects of the situation was relatively simple: the faculty member had broken the law and the travel agent could choose to press charges. If, however, the travel agent chose *not* to pursue his legal options, then what was the president to do? This faculty member had been at the college for over twenty years and was a tenured professor. Her hands could be slapped and she could be warned that if she ever stepped out of line again she would be punished; she could be fired on the spot and the president would face a variety of union actions in her defense, or risk her personally filing a law suit against the college. Even though the president was sure the college would ultimately prevail, it would be expensive and the source of lots of juicy stories in the local newspaper. Finally, the president could choose to seek some compromise that would be acceptable in the long run yet not compromise an institutional, or personal value. The third route was eventually the one chosen. The faculty member was suspended without pay for a period of time until she was eligible to retire from the state system and start collecting a pension. The president later admitted that the personal preference at first was to fire her on the spot for violating an institutional trust and for being so selfishly stupid. However, the president realized that any personal desire for revenge or for exercising position power must be given up in favor of the more objective criteria. What would be fair? What would be best for the institution? What would serve as a strong message to the offender, as well as to others who might be tempted to use the institution's name in a similar fashion, or to do something else that was basically dishonest? There was concern that the willingness to reach a compromise position would be seen by some as being unethical, but the president never really considered the possibility that anyone else at the college would have wanted the whole situation ignored. Therefore, the concern for behaving ethically didn't have a lot to do with "right or wrong;" that part was clear. The concern for ethics was less clear cut, which is what all ethical discussions ultimately come down to: once the right or wrong of an issue has been decided or discovered, then what does the president do about it?

In an article printed in the AAWCJC *Journal* in 1992, Elaine Johnson of Mt. Hood Community College states the issue as follows:

> Presumably, the leader's responsibility ought always to be to uphold principles which safeguard the rights of those accountable to them.
>
> Presumably, it is the leader's responsibility, then, to honor obligations arising from relationships between employer and employee, teacher and student, administrator and faculty member. It is, furthermore, the leaders' responsibility to dignify all persons in an organization by appreciating their work, giving them their due, being compassionate, tolerant, and fair.
>
> Surely leaders ought to behave this way. Leaders must also judge. It is their responsibility to make ethical judgments. If they refuse judgments, they are tacitly condoning them...
>
> The basis of ethical judgments must quite simply be the truth that people are by definition valuable. From that single objective truth springs a world of oughts and shoulds that can guide us as individuals and guide us as leaders in our work. (p. 11)

Institutional Concerns

Even though no one else in the institution may think of it, the president ultimately has to put every issue in a broader context of what is right and best for the institution. This is the most difficult perspective to main-

tain, but also perhaps the most important. The president is the only advocate for the whole institution — everyone else has the luxury of being an
advocate for his or her particular program or realm of responsibility. The
president really does not have that option.

Presidential ethics are comprised of fairness, balance, and objectivity.
The ethical questions usually discussed involve definitions of what is moral,
or what is right or wrong, or what is possible. Those are important consid-
erations, but in the long run the more complex decisions we have to make
can become so ambiguous that we have to force ourselves to step back and
remain more impersonal in order to do what is ethically sound.

Changes in the Perception of Ethical Behavior

Ethics as applied to the individual president is the topic which has
received much more notoriety than those issues just discussed. Countless
examples can be given which span our community college history about
the president who was fired for taking bribes, or for making questionable
political contributions, or for diverting institutional funds or personnel for
individual use. Unfortunately presidents have, on occasion, been caught
shoplifting or have become embroiled in personal family disasters of one
kind or another which have become public embarrassments to the college.

Because of such instances in which public officials have been less than
trustworthy, many states have implemented ethics panels which review
financial information about the officials and are empowered to investigate
any alleged breach of the state's ethical code. It is not unusual for a public
college president to have to sign notarized forms disclosing financial information not only on the president but also on the president's family. Apparently we are not trusted to behave "ethically".

More important, however, is that the perception of what **is** ethical behavior has changed over the years. In 1970 it may not have been considered unethical for a college president to accept a generous gift, or expensive tickets to some event, from someone with whom the college had a
relationship. Now that same action would put the president in jeopardy of
being fired unless some ingenious explanation was offered and accepted.
The rules have changed dramatically. As a result, a president who is perceived as being even slightly unethical, or of using poor judgment about a
personal situation, loses effectiveness as a leader demanding ethical behavior or standards of other college employees and students. While the
standards vary from college to college, any president who can live by the
motto, "When in doubt, don't," will probably remain effective. Another
deterrent to temptation is to imagine how one's actions might be explained
in the headlines of the local newspaper. In essence, ethics, both institutional and personal, fall into that great category of "I don't know how to

define it, but I know it when I see it" which has been used to describe other thorny social topics, such as pornography. We must be aware of ethics, we must care about ethics, and we must talk about ethics. Some day, then, perhaps we will be able to define ethics as well.

4

Gender and Ethnicity

When I first became a president and was being interviewed frequently, among the many questions I was asked was, "How does it feel to be a woman president?" My answer was borrowed from Rep. Patricia Schroeder of Colorado who answered that kind of question by saying, "I don't know, I have never been a man in this position." At the heart of the question, regardless of the seemingly flippant answer, is a dilemma that has plagued many as women have become more visible in positions of leadership and authority in our culture. Are we different? Is our leadership style different? Can we be as "effective" as white males have been over the centuries? Are we accepted by those whom we are supposed to be leading? This society has not yet reached the point of being able to view women and minority leaders in any segment of life as a normal occurrence; we are still the exception, sometimes the token, and always somewhat on display.

Even so, the record in community colleges of providing opportunities for women and minorities is better than in any other segment of higher education. Those of us who have benefited from the chances available to us can talk at length about the struggles to be seen as equal or the doors that were closed because of race or gender, or the battles that were, and are, being fought just to have multiple points of view represented on the educational agenda.

Whether or not the presence of women in decision-making and leadership roles has made a difference in the organization is still being debated. For example, there were eleven female public community college presidents in 1975 and one hundred and six in 1992 (ACE, Office of Women in Higher Education). That means that still less than 15 % of our public community colleges are being led by women, hardly enough of a cohort, some could argue, to discover broad based changes based on differences between genders.

There have been changes in how organizations are perceived, in how effectiveness is measured, and in how leadership is evaluated. Some of those changes have been brought about by economic conditions which have seen the emergence of the global economy with its increased competition; some changes have been spurred on by rapidly changing technology, which itself requires flexibility and innovation; and some changes which have flattened organizations and decentralized decision-making have occurred out of the sheer necessity to trim the workforce and operate more efficiently. The fact that these types of changes have occurred at the same moment in history that more women have entered the workforce and have also achieved positions of authority and influence is just coincidental. Or is it?

WHERE WE HAVE BEEN

Many of the books written about life in corporate America in the seventies and early eighties gave women advice about how to dress and behave in order to fit into a male-dominated and controlled world. The assumption was that life would always be lived in a military-type hierarchy, and the machine bureaucracy model was still dominant. Many of the assumptions of the business world were also present in education, which was itself a male-dominated segment of society. Women believed—and were encouraged to believe—that their ways of thinking or doing or knowing had no place in the corporation or the college. We were told that because we did not have the experience of the military or of team sports that our upbringing was deficient and would therefore prevent us from achieving "power" and "success" until we could learn to think and behave like men. Institutional and corporate practices, which had systematically excluded women and minorities from positions of influence and control, were not seen as the essence of the problem. Rather, the women who aspired to those positions of influence and control were viewed as the problem. Thus, in the seventies and eighties we were spending a great deal of time and energy developing seminars and workshops for women to teach them how to survive in the male-dominated world.

It is now more recognized that women's needs are no different from men's needs in the arena of developing "leadership skills." For example, leaders must be able to: work effectively with people; make decisions; fine tune their political and budgeting skills; and to operate at a fairly high level of intellectual functioning in order to evaluate issues, anticipate and plan for the future. Gender and race are irrelevant in the development of individual leadership potential, though they seem still to have some relevance in the workplace where those skills are put into practice.

One of the clichés of the early women's movement was that men were hired and promoted for their potential, and women were hired or promoted because of their accomplishments. Women had to prove their capabilities and document their triumphs in order to be seen as capable while the slightest misstep or failure was an indictment of the entire gender. The sad reality is that even now that attitude still exists in many organizations, not excluding community colleges. Why is it that fewer than 15% of our community college presidents are female when it has been documented that well over 60% of our students are female and at least half of our faculties and staffs are female? What is happening to all of that talent and potential for leadership?

Unfortunately, the answer is obvious. Gender discrimination is still a reality in higher education, it is still pervasive, and it still exists in some form in all institutions (Green, 1988). It has been easy to identify some forms of discrimination, such as salary inequities, or different rates of promotion between genders, or curricula which do not recognize the writings or contributions of women over the centuries. Those issues have been widely attacked, and some changes are occurring when discrepancies are discovered. However, the more subtle forms of gender discrimination are still hard to address. One good example is pointed out by Donna Shavlik and Judith Touchton in Green's *Leaders for a New Era.* They state that women must remember that they may often be treated as a class rather than as individuals with strengths and weaknesses. For example, the stereotype that women are not good in math may impede the career progress of women as administrative and budget officers. Or another stereotype that women are not willing to move in order to advance professionally may keep some well-qualified female candidates out of circulation unfairly. As already discussed in an earlier chapter, mobility—or the lack of it—is no longer a gender issue, and the assumptions of the past must be eradicated.

Women are viewed as representatives of a class. When one of us succeeds, especially as a president, we breathe a sigh of relief. When one of us fails, we know the unenlightened institutional response may be, "We tried a woman in that position and she failed; therefore, we should not try that again." An additional paradox is that if we do well, we are the exception. If we fail, we have remained representative of the class. I do not know of any circumstances in which that same standard is applied to my male colleagues.

Two more points must be made on this most difficult topic, however. The first is that we all know women and men, who place every experience, every achievement, every setback in the realm of gender or race: "I would have been selected for Position A but for the fact that I am a woman/minority;" or, "They wouldn't treat me this way if I were white/male;" or, "The only reason that so-and-so was promoted is because she is a woman

and it is the white males of the world who are being discriminated against."
Sometimes those perceptions are true, but not always. Gender and race
have been used as excuses by those who have other issues about which
they should be more concerned, such as basic competence. However, as
long as this society is going to use race and gender as a way of differentiat-
ing or stereotyping individuals, then there will be persons who will turn
that societal inclination inside-out, using it whenever necessary to justify
failure or to save face.

WHERE WE NEED TO GO

The second point is that in addition to simply recognizing that women
and minorities have had to fight an uphill battle to progress toward professional parity, even in higher education, we must add another dimension to
the debate. It is not enough that we have spent years learning to work with
white males; we need now to help them learn to work with us as their
colleagues. This goes back to a generalization made earlier that men have,
for the most part, expected women to change to fit into their world. Instead, the world has changed. Workers now must scramble to learn how to
behave differently, and they may see their carefully crafted worlds spin
out of control. In *Reinventing the Corporation* by John Naisbett and Patricia
Aburdene is a statement, "Significant change occurs when there is a
confluence of changing values and economic necessity" (p.51). We know
now that the economic necessity for change is upon us, and it looks as
though, finally, many values thought to be more "feminine" than "masculine" are going to be the ones which lead us out of crisis and into a new
century. Therefore, it is up to us who have entered the professional world
to help those who were here before us learn from us.

ANDROGYNY

As early as 1981, Alice Sargent was writing about the concept of androgyny in management, suggesting that there was an increasing research
base which indicated that it made for happier people as well as for better
managers. Her explanation of androgyny, which forces organizations to
focus on interdependence and mutual support," heralds a new era for organizations and for workers in both their professional and personal lives.
The spirit of this era is a concern for people—though not at the expense of
productivity—and a concern for significant changes in interpersonal relationships between men and women in all sorts of configurations, as bosses
and subordinates, and as peers." (p.13)

Androgyny has been seen as the ultimate blend of the masculine and
feminine. This blend can create a functional, productive, yet compassion-

ate organization. To achieve androgyny, the organization must still focus on the more traditional concerns—planning, organizing, delegating, evaluating—while at the same time coming to grips with other issues, such as how people work together effectively, how to meet the need for support systems, or how to deal with emotions and dependency (Sargent, 1981). Those characteristics on the first list have traditionally been seen as "masculine", while the issues mentioned in the second list are traditionally "feminine". Many don't stop to think about behavior in these terms because gender-related behavior expectations are deeply and invisibly imbedded in our society. While it may be true that many changes have taken place that were only anticipated by Sargent in 1981, and that many organizations today are closer to androgyny than they were then, there are still discernible differences between how men and women behave in organizations.

GENDER DIFFERENCES IN MANAGEMENT

An important study of women as managers and leaders was done by Sally Helgesen. In her book, *The Female Advantage: Women's Ways of Leadership* (1990), she studied four women CEOs to discover what made them successful and how—if at all—they differed from their male counterparts. She then compared her women and their leadership styles to those described by Mintzberg when he did his exhaustive study of managers in *The Nature of Managerial Work* (1973). Mintzberg reached eight major conclusions about managers (all male, as they would have been in 1973):

1. They worked relentlessly, taking no breaks in their activities during the day.

2. Their typical days were fragmented because so much of their time was spent "putting out fires."

3. They had little, if any, time for anything not directly related to their work. This included family time.

4. They always preferred face to face encounters and spent 60% of their time in scheduled meetings. However, this led to a preoccupation with scheduling and "time management".

5. Time outside the office was also spent representing their companies, so that 22 to 38% of their time was spent with colleagues or clients gathering information for the benefit of the company.

6. The fast pace and constant interruptions left them little, if any, time for contemplation or reflection.

7. They often felt that they could not distinguish their identities from their positions.

8. Finally, all of them had difficulty sharing information, seeing it as a power source which needed to be guarded so that they would not lose their competitive edge.

Helgesen described the women she studied in this way:

1. They worked a "steady pace" but did schedule breaks during the day.

2. Unscheduled tasks or encounters were not seen as interruptions; the women made a conscious effort to be accessible and easily ap proachable.

3. Not all of their outside activities were directly related to their work.

4. They also preferred face to face meetings or encounters, but that did not prevent them from scheduling time to open the mail, which they saw as part of communicating with others and remaining in personal touch.

5. They had a web of relationships outside the organization, similar to the men Mintzberg studied.

6. They concentrated on long range issues and trends and kept a broad focus in order to monitor where their own companies fit into the "big picture." Helgesen calls this focusing on the "ecology of lead ership." (p.26)

7. They viewed their jobs as but one facet of their identity, rather than their entire being.

8. A planned part of every day was reserved for the sharing of infor mation with colleagues.

It is apparent from Helgesen's conclusions that the leadership and management styles of the men and women were very different. Those dif ferences in what women and men have been taught to value gets trans lated into the workplace. Traditional male values have included compet ing, with the goal being to win; making rules and living within bound aries and following procedures; and submerging individuality for the greater good. In contrast, women have learned to depend on cooperation and relationships; to disregard or disdain rules or structures which are au thoritarian; and to abandon concepts of victory or winning when those values threaten the harmony of the whole group with whom they feel a connection. Thus women value caring, intuitive decision-making, social responsibility and ethics, and keeping work and business in its proper perspective with other important life activity. These "feminine" principles have been embraced because businesses need them in order to survive. What we finally come closer to achieving is an androgynous workplace.

Research continues to show that men and women see the world differently, respond to it differently, and communicate about it differently. Gender differences are not just a figment of the feminist imagination; they are real and abiding. The presence of more women at all levels of the organization, but especially at the upper hierarchical levels, has brought about some profound changes. It has also brought some very complex problems to the fore.

There has been an enormous shift in thinking about some issues: child care, sexual harassment, flexible work schedules, mobility of families, the bottom line and achieving short term results at the expense of long term stability, health care, multiculturalism and diversity, the definition of success, and quality of life. The world has been turned on its side; many of the traditional values and rules of the world previously dominated and controlled by white males have been altered. Even Tom Peters, the guru of excellence in the 1980s, has abandoned his jingoism about quality corporate America and lectures now about "the compassionate organization."

THE IMPACT IN COMMUNITY COLLEGES

For the community college, the elements necessary for institutional, and therefore presidential success, are cooperation, collaboration, creativity, inclusion, and process. In her landmark book *In a Different Voice*, Carol Gilligan outlined some of the differences between the way women and men make decisions. She found that women are more likely to base their choices on the impact those choices may have on others—on their relationships. Cooperation and collaboration are important; before a leader can make a good choice for an organization, she must examine the impact it will have on others. The best way to do that is to get input, to make sure that there is an inclusive process for information and opinion gathering. In hierarchical organizations—which community colleges still are—getting people to work together and to listen to each others' points of view is a time-consuming task. It is also arduous and occasionally frustrating. For all of our talk about collegiality in higher education, there are more examples of competitive behavior and top-down decision-making processes than there are of true cooperation and collaboration. Gilligan's assertions about how women make decisions, however, could lead us to believe that women are naturally inclined toward collegial leadership styles because of their emphasis on relationships with others and wanting to make sure that everyone is at least partially happy.

The other conclusion that Gilligan reached is that for the most part, men are more inclined to make decisions based on abstract concepts of justice or "rightness": following the rules, adhering to convention, playing the game the way it is supposed to be played based on some external determination of what the rules are. As leaders, men who use these guidelines in decision-making may be less inclined to value process or cooperation since the guidelines are established and the rules clear. Additionally, this thought mode generally values competition more than collaboration, believing that results are achieved through the competitive process. If the competitive process doesn't lead to clear winners or losers, then we have the court system to adjudicate disputes and rule on "what is right." Consensus, which is generally the goal of collaboration, is not a popular concept with "justice" oriented thinkers. It is too fuzzy and, again, too slow.

It should be obvious that saying women think in one way and men in another is an insupportable statement, as is the belief that women lead in one way and men in another. However, what is supportable is that many respected researchers in addition to Gilligan or Helgesen have reached the same conclusion: there are significant differences generally in how men and women see the world and try to solve problems. These differences are getting translated more and more into the workplace as women have the opportunity to lead and be role models for organizations. Thus, we are indeed getting closer to achieving androgyny: blending the best of both genders to create the organizations which will be able to adapt to an uncertain future. Female leaders have had to learn from male leaders the value of decisiveness, the value of structure, and the value of watchfulness. And from female leaders, male leaders have had to learn the value of listening, the value of creativity, and the value of the personal touch.

There are still so few women, comparatively speaking, in community college presidencies that the temptation to adopt traditional styles of behavior and old patterns is great indeed. In addition, boards are not often used to working with women, nor are other community leaders. A subtle and insidious sexism can still exist for the female president, and she must be aware of how it affects how she is perceived and how she is heard. Most women who have become presidents have probably adapted to certain types of behavior and have figured out when to confront blatant sexism and when to leave it alone. Most of the time, we do not confront directly. The catch-22 for us is that as women we are sensitive to gender issues and are not willingly submissive or passive by nature. On the other hand, as presidents we represent our institutions, and our actions and words are heard more loudly. The dilemma, therefore, is whether or not to risk offending someone who is sexist or racist, probably without being aware of it. As stated earlier, the president is judged by his or her symbolic value as well as by actual accomplishments. If the president starts to gain a reputation in the community for being confrontational on gender issues, then she risks losing her effectiveness as a spokesperson for the institution. Nonetheless, it is the responsibility of the president as the academic leader and educator to help others see that their exclusionary attitudes are harmful and unjustified. She must support efforts to broaden the academic experience for students and to make sure that minority points of view are presented with equal validity and emphasis. She must work in the community to make sure that other women's voices are heard and that women are included in the decision-making circles. She must make sure that the language others use and that which she uses herself is inclusive and free of bias.

The American Council on Education, Office of Women in Higher Education sponsored a national "summit" of women college presidents in celebration of its twentieth year of existence. The summit, which was actually the second one convened, was devoted to the development of a "blueprint" for action so that the concerns of women who are leaders in this segment of our society would become more prominent on national and global agendas. As stated by Donna Shavlik and Judith Touchton, "...the visibility of women in the public domain has not meant that the power of our voices has become manifest in the fundamental organizing principles of our society, or in the setting of our institutional, national, and global agendas." (1994). They urge each woman who is a college president, either working alone or with groups of other women who are presidents, to make their voices heard on a variety of educational and social issues which impact everyone's lives regardless of gender. Women who are community college presidents must continue to take their roles very seriously for all of the reasons outlined by Shavlik and Touchton: we are still the minority, but we are in a position to have some influence in our own communities and on our own campuses in the creation of a more humane future.

I long for the day when I am not the only woman in a meeting of community leaders, or one of two or three women in meetings of dozens of college presidents. And I know that it is my responsibility to make those desires be realized by mentoring other women, by being prepared and doing my job well so that all women do not lose credibility due to my failures or mistakes. As much as I welcome changes in attitudes and in what kind of behavior is valued in organizations, I also know that it is still an uphill battle for all of us to free ourselves from our own biases, many of which are gender-related. How are we going to help our students prepare for the future if we are willing to let subtle forms of discrimination exist in our colleges? How can we justify academic programs which make no attempt to break down stereotypic barriers—such as few males in our nursing programs or few women in our engineering programs, either as professors or students?

The president must actively address these types of patterns and not simply shrug them off as "unavoidable." The excuse that has been used for decades to exclude women and minorities from certain professions is that there are not enough qualified candidates and that we refuse to lower standards. As open door institutions, community colleges serve the previously disenfranchised and are proud to say that more minorities and women attend our institutions than attend baccalaureate institutions. If we really want to change the world, we will bring back some of those students and hire them to be our teachers and our counselors and our deans and our presidents. The time has come for there to be no more excuses from either gender of community college leader. We don't have time to waste.

Essay

WHAT'S IT LIKE BEING THE ONLY BLACK WOMAN HERE?
by Belle Wheelan

"What's it like being the only black (or woman) here?" "Have you ever experienced discrimination?" "Has being a black or a woman helped or hurt your chances in getting a job?"

These are just examples of questions that minorities and women who have achieved some level of success are repeatedly asked. Often, I am tempted to respond with such mundane responses as "It feels natural," "If I have, people have been smart enough not to let me know that I've been," and "You'd have to ask the people who actually hired me."

There is no doubt that the revolution of the 60s made it possible for the massive increase in the numbers of minorities and women to now hold positions of responsibility in major organizations today. Prior to the civil rights legislation of the 60s, minorities were seldom seen in such positions as college presidents, vice-presidents or deans of instruction, or in the area of financial administration. More often than not, Hispanic-Americans were found teaching Spanish, African-Americans were found teaching history, sociology or physical education, etc.

Today, institutions of higher education are recognizing that in order to retain students from diverse backgrounds, there must be representation within the professional ranks from the ethnic groups that the students represent. Support services for minorities on predominately white campuses often make the difference between students leaving or transferring after one semester and their retention through to graduation.

Having been a minority student on a predominately white campus during my undergraduate years, I am aware of the pain in having been one of only a handful. Nowhere in the administration or faculty ranks was an African American to be found. The few of us had to support each other. We hung together. We ate together, sat together at athletic events, cried over broken relationships, etc. While I don't think my fellow students ever treated me differently because of my ethnicity, there were times when I felt as if the differences in our experiences created an artificial chasm between us that made communication and socialization difficult. We had to make a conscious effort to find common ground among us.

Today, when I am asked what it's like to be different, it is still difficult to put those insecurities and fears from the past into words. The difficulty comes from not wanting to seem like a crusader for underdogs. I don't want to leave the impression that minorities or women want pity or special treatment. On the contrary, we want only an opportunity to compete fairly with the masses. At no time do we want to feel that we are perceived to hold the positions we do because we are minorities or because we are women.

As I walk the halls at my college and visit with students, I make it a point to talk with *all* students and to get *all* students talking with each other. I make it a point to hire qualified people of *all* ethnic groups and both genders so that appropriate support and role models are available for our students.

There is no denying that there are behavioral and cultural differences between genders or among ethnic groups. Instead of those differences creating barriers, however, it is imperative that organizational leaders make every attempt to help people appreciate those differences and learn from them. We must celebrate and share those differences with each other.

There was a great deal of concern within my current institution when I let it be known that we would not celebrate Black History Month at the college. I'm sure that people assumed that since I am African American, I would increase the activities during February. Instead, we celebrate Cultural Diversity Month during February. The reason for this has little to do with the fact that I am trying to ensure that all cultures are provided an opportunity to be recognized on campus. It is because I refuse to relegate the celebration of my heritage to one month a year. In our activities program, we make a conscious effort to expose our students and staff to the richness that is provided by the contributions of women and all minority groups to this great land.

The challenge of creating an air of appreciation for diversity, while not putting people off because they feel diversity has been pushed down their throat, is a great one. For a person to be the leader of an organization and to be a woman or member of an ethnic group presents an additional challenge. It is difficult to persuade people that you are merely doing what is right, not just what you want to do. But since that expectation is there for us to take the lead in ensuring the celebration of diversity, we must accept that challenge.

To insist that courses include discussions of varying viewpoints resulting from gender or ethnic differences, that applications for positions be kept open until the pool is representative, or that we make no assumptions about the ability level of students because of their gender or ethnic background, are all difficult to do if you too are a member of a different gender of ethnic group than the one you're trying to persuade. But the battle must be fought.

In delivering speeches to various groups throughout my service area,

I find myself carrying the banner for both women and ethnic minorities. I accept the challenge to do that because I want people to know that we are real people with real feelings. We are not all that different. We want the same things for our children that they do. We eat the same foods, shop in the same stores, practice the same or similar religions.

I share my experiences growing up in a city that was 57% minority (50% Hispanic and 7% African American), while experiencing little turmoil in the 60s when compared to other cities. In those days, the differences were between blacks and whites. If you weren't black, you were white even if you were Hispanic, Asian, Native American, etc. While integration occurred with little disruption to our lives, we did witness the turmoil in other parts of the country.

In 1964, I was a twelve year old eighth grader in a Catholic school about to go to the white Catholic high school. My teacher brought a television to class so that we could see the footage of the riots in other cities and she could help us understand what was happening to people who looked like us. She told us two things that I share in every speech I give because I feel it is as relevant today as it was then, though with a different application. She told us first, that black people (we were black then) were obviously the most important people in the world—otherwise, white folks wouldn't be making such a big deal over us. Today, I translate that to mean that, regardless of your gender or ethnicity, whenever you are prepared and trying to get ahead and people are trying to keep you back, it means they are afraid you are going to take something away from them...that you are important or they wouldn't be putting up such a battle to keep you down.

The second thing she told us was that, regardless of the color of any of our skin, we were all Americans. And that American ends in the letters i-c-a-n, *I CAN*, and that she didn't want to ever hear us say what we could not do until we had tried. As African-Americans, I tell audiences we doubly can because both words end in i-c-a-n.

Today, I still find strength and encouragement from these lessons. As I communicate with other women and African-American presidents, I find that I am not alone. We are all in positions where "being lonely at the top" takes on an entirely new meaning when you are female or black, brown, etc. While we have reached the pinnacle of our professions, we are still minorities and are often perceived to be women or minorities first and leaders second. It is something we have grown to accept and with which we each deal differently. While there are folks out there who will question the decisions I make based on my gender or ethnicity, I accept the fact that that is their problem, not mine.

I recognize more and more each day that I am indeed from a different generation, and I strive to understand the frustration and anger of the current generation who feel that the dream has died. The parents of the children of the 60s were products of the Depression. They vowed that their children would never have to do without anything, and they worked hard to give us what we wanted. There was a strong work ethic that was passed from them to us, that if we worked hard, we would realize the American dream. Somewhere along the line, we as parents have let our children down.

We have forgotten to pass on the work ethic along with the things that our children have requested. We have given them so much that they feel as if someone is supposed to keep on giving. Additionally, they want it right away. Immediate gratification is the name of the game. Unfortunately, for many minorities, the role models they are emulating are sports figures and drug addicts who get the publicity for achieving fame and fortune immediately.

As women and minorities, we have a challenge to get out from behind our desks in our plush offices and go back and visit the 'hood.' We must let them know that true success is not measured in how quickly you can achieve greatness, but in how you go about achieving it to ensure it lasts. The fight today is different than it was in the 60s, but it is still a major battle. We must begin to provide encouragement and role models early in elementary school.

Those women who first entered the nontraditional areas of work in the 60s and 70s must also visit schools to let the girls know that there are career opportunities for them. Members of minority groups must take a moment to let children know that goals can be achieved only through academic preparation—that while it might take a while to achieve what we want, the end result is worth the work.

Like all people, every woman and every minority has a different way of coping with the alienation, frustration, criticism, etc. they experience. No two women nor two minorities may have the same strategies simply because of those characteristics. We are all unique. I hope I am around when such differences cease being excuses for us living together as one people, when, to paraphrase Dr. King, "… people will be judged by the content of their character and not the color of their skin or their gender." I can only hope.

Belle Wheelan is President of Central Virginia College in Lynchburg, VA. When she was appointed to that position in 1992, she became the first African American woman in Virginia higher education to hold a position at that level. She has served as a member of the American Association of Community Colleges' Board of Directors

Essay

GENDER, ETHNICITY, AND LEADERSHIP
by Leila Gonzalez-Sullivan

I always wonder why after five years in the position I still hesitate or stumble over the response "I'm a college president" when someone asks me what I do for a living. Is it because even now few women hold such positions? Is it because modesty was strongly emphasized in my up-bringing as a child of Puerto Rican background? Is it because of some insecurity about my own talents and skills that I haven't yet overcome? Probably all of the above and none of the above at the same time.

I am very proud of what I have achieved in my professional life, and at this point in my career I feel confident of my abilities and judgment without need to prove myself. If someone were to ask me what marks the "Sullivan years" at my college, I could answer with real accomplishments that have changed the direction of the institution and made a difference in people's lives. So why the hesitation? Most likely because I am growing weary of the reaction to my answer: the questioners still respond most often with surprise or even confusion at the idea of a college president who is female and Puerto Rican, in spite of the current emphasis on multiculturalism and diversity and gender issues. And there is a part of me that wishes to be seen simply as an individual rather than a symbol or a token, holder of a job title with several modifiers. There is another part of me, however, which takes very seriously the opportunity to inform and teach others about the status and achievements of those groups.

Over the past few years there have been a series of research projects on minority women who have become college presidents, and these have encouraged me to analyze my own career trajectory in the context of my gender and ethnic background. Interestingly, most of the studies, such as the 1992 dissertation by Lois Knowlton, have found that there aren't many common themes in the lives of the few Hispanic women who have reached the community college presidency. We come from various countries and economic backgrounds. Some of us had strong mothers, or parents with higher educational levels. There are those who were born in the United States and those who were not. For some, Spanish is a second rather than a first language, although we are all bilingual. We range from first born to last born and represent the full spectrum of religions and politics. Some of us have felt discrimination. While it is true that we have in common our gender, our Latin American roots, and our involvement with community colleges, we are each unique individuals who have reached the presidency through considerably different routes.

How did I get to where I am today? Was it a factor of my gender or ethnicity? Did I have some grand plan for career achievement? I have to confess that it was none of these. Rather, I seem to have traveled a zigzag path, taking advantage of opportunities as they appeared, learning as much from the mistakes as the successes and banging my head against quite a few brick walls in the process. Only now am I beginning to see patterns with my 20/20 hindsight.

A fair analysis would show that my gender and ethnicity did, in fact, have a lot to do with my choices and that the two characteristics were and still are intertwined. Some personal history would probably be helpful at this point. I was born here in the States of a Puerto Rican father and an Iowan mother. For many reasons, my father chose not to live on the island, but our lifestyle and values were clearly shaped by his background, especially his deep religious convictions. Like many Latinos, we traveled back and forth to San Juan frequently and often had Puerto Rican relatives visiting or living with us for periods of time, so I moved comfortably between the mainland and island environments and spoke Spanish with relative fluency, although it was not my first language. My role as a girl and the oldest child was clear: to be obedient, responsible, discreet, and studious. Growing up in the U.S., I was often impatient with the restrictions imposed by my father because "that's how it is done in Puerto Rico" or "girls don't do that on the island." I honestly don't remember any overt discrimination based on our Puerto Rican background, even though some of my relatives worked in the garment industry in New York and were probably viewed as poor immigrants by others.

To these childhood experiences I attribute many of the enduring themes in my life: a love of languages as a means of enhancing the ability to express oneself; a feeling of great pride in being Puerto Rican; an appreciation of cultural differences and extended families; a love of color and music and celebrations; a strong sense of social and civic responsibility; and the conviction that education is still the best means to a fulfilling life and that all people should be treated with respect and justice. These were all strong and proud messages which served as the foundation for my adult actions.

At the same time, I received the typical messages of my generation about gender: girls should use their education to support their husband's careers; girls should achieve, but not so much that they overshadow boys; girls don't do well in math and science; girls should be responsible and self-sacrificing; traditional jobs such as teaching and nursing are good choices until a girl gets married. It is also important to throw into this mix of ethnic and gender stuff, the fact that I was a college student in the 60s and absorbed the messages of liberal politics, social action, civil rights, and resistance to the Vietnam War.

How this young girl of Puerto Rican extraction, a '60s idealist, arrived at the doorstep of a community college was happily accidental. After marriage, the birth of a child, and a move to South Carolina, I was unable to find a job in my chosen field of librarianship and so I became a teacher of reading skills in a small, church-related Black college. Soon after that, I accepted a position at the local two-year college and became a department chair as well as an instructor, all with no formal training in either administration or teaching.

From the time of that first job in a community college, a series of experiences I call "epiphanies" marked my movement upward through the ranks to my present position, each one shaping and clarifying my values and philosophy. The lessons learned from each of these experiences, even the negative ones, have enriched and guided many of my actions since then, particularly as an administrator. As a result of these I also became hooked on community colleges.

The first "epiphany" occurred at that college in South Carolina where, after two successful years as department chair, I was bypassed for a promotion in favor of a 70-year-old white male with a doctorate and proven record of inaction and underachievement. I don't think I recognized this as sex and age discrimination at the time, thinking rather that my lack of credentials was what was holding me back. This was particularly ironic in view of my involvement in the early feminist movement at that point.

After moving to Arkansas and completing a doctorate, we returned to the East Coast and I resumed my career in an urban community college, again working as a reading teacher and chairperson of the Developmental Studies Department. I also became active in an organization of Hispanic professionals working to promote Hispanic opportunities and rights in higher education. Here my commitment to women's rights became linked with my identification as a Latina.

During this period, three events stand out as significant and formative "epiphanies" again. In the first instance, an administrative decision was made at the "open door" college to impose different entrance standards for non-English speakers than for others, in effect excluding many minority. Eventually I chose to oppose this decision publicly after internal means failed to correct the situation. This was not the best move for my career. Looking back on the episode now from a president's perspective, it seems an unfortunate mix of poor administration, miscommunication among the various parties, and lack of political savvy on the part of a relatively inexperienced middle manager. Certainly, I learned a great deal about process, communication, and resistance from that experience that has applications in my work today.

A second "epiphany" occurred when I was encouraged by that same president to apply for the Leaders of the '80s program sponsored by the Maricopa Community Colleges, the League for Innovation, and the American Association of Women in Community and Junior Colleges. Because there were extremely few women and minorities in positions of leadership in community colleges in the '70s and '80s, this FIPSE-funded program had been developed to prepare women for presidencies. This is not to say that I had ever considered the possibility of a presidency. My most daring aspiration at that moment was to be an academic dean someday, and I had made no real plans to move in that direction. As a result of my attendance at Leaders, however, a new world opened up and the presidency became my goal. I was also introduced to the concept of different leadership styles and to research on the psychology of women, both of which have been incorporated into my own activities over the years. More than any other experience, I view the Leaders Program as the turning point in my career.

Yet another "epiphany" can be attributed to that institution. My commitment to women's rights became highly personal when I realized that I was being paid several thousand dollars less than male administrators with comparable responsibilities. I chose to take legal action and eventually was able to resolve the problem, but in the course of events I learned that legal actions are extremely costly in psychological as well as financial terms. I would probably make the same choice in the same circumstances today but perhaps I would have a better sense of the consequences. This experience has also made me deeply sensitive to the personal anguish resulting from labor disputes and changes in employment such as reassignments and layoffs. While as an administrator I might still have to make difficult decisions affecting people's work, I hope I am attentive to the emotional and personal consequences of such decisions as well.

One final experience is noteworthy in this chronicle, illustrating as it does an often ignored aspect of cultural differences. Most Americans continue to view Latinos as an amorphous group characterized primarily by a common language. The divisions and differences among Latinos are seldom acknowledged, yet they frequently affected the operations of another institution where I worked for several years. This college had Cubans supervising certain academic programs, Puerto Ricans predominantly in some administrative services, and an influx of Central American students with new habits and perspectives that confused just about everyone. These groups were quite different by nationality and culture and clearly had different agendas at the college. As chief academic officer, I had to understand and cope with these differences in order to move our programs forward.

I also thought it advantageous to speak Spanish and relate to these groups based on my Puerto Rican background. It was a real jolt, then, when a Puerto Rican colleague explained that because I wasn't born on the island, many of the staff members and some of my professional associates did not view me as truly Latino. It took considerable introspection to accept my status as a second-generation Hispanic who could never be "born of the island." I have since come to value exactly what I am: a person of Latin American background who has grown up in the culture of this country and for whom the island culture will always be somewhat alien. In this context, I appreciate my roots and can play an important role in promoting Latino rights and opportunities without trying to be something I am not.

There have been other pivotal events in my career, moments of great learning and strong feelings, but the ones described above offer the best illustration of what influenced and shaped this particular college president outside the realm of formal training. These "epiphanies" also illustrate the types of experiences that have made me a crusader for women's and minority rights.

To conclude this essay, I would offer a few cautions in relation to ethnicity and gender and leadership. First of all, there may be a greater expectation that minority leaders will espouse affirmative action principles, just as I expected the president of that one institution to be a champion of non-English speakers. It is important to recall that members of ethnic and racial groups have biases and prejudices like anyone else and that most leaders—minority or not—strive for balance and objectivity regardless of their personal commitments. One would hope that minority presidents are held to the same—not higher or different— standards in affirmative action and other matters.

That, of course, leads to the second issue—tokenism. It is difficult to accept that one is often included in a candidate pool or panel of speakers or committee only because of one's skin color or surname. At the same time, there is a certain sense of advantage in being a minority during a period when many institutions are making strides in affirmative action. There may also be a sense of responsibility to represent one's group well. I yearn for the day when gender and ethnicity will simply not matter and each of us will be seen as individuals. In the meantime, however, I intend to use my status as a token firmly, believing as I do that once my foot is in the door, my mouth is right behind.

Yet a third issue involves the current emphasis on different leadership styles as these might relate to gender. Heaven knows I would like to be a leader such as Carol Gilligan describes: supportive of others, attentive to process, inclusive in decision-making. I would love to avoid "female" communication styles that appear weak and ineffective, speaking with a level of authority that males might understand, as Deborah Tannen suggests. I could even buy into Peters' MBWA and TQM and CQI and the rest of the alphabet. Perhaps if I had possessed these qualities and skill I could have resolved some of the "epiphanies" described above differently, but some of them took long years to develop and others are simply not in my nature.

I am frankly leery of the current psychologizing of management theory, particularly since many of the popular books of the moment propose their theories in terms of dichotomies, either-ors that don't seem to fit the complexities of most organizations or personalities. No leader wants to admit openly that he or she is insensitive or uninterested in people, or dictatorial, or a poor communicator, yet those often seem to be the choices in such dichotomous theories. The best approach seems to be flexibility, or what I call eclectic leadership, adopting those techniques which seem useful, trying to be sensitive to the human dimensions of each problem, moving among leadership styles as the circumstances demand and not flagellating oneself for those times when one must make decisions in rather authoritarian fashion. Women moving into leadership positions in higher education must be very careful not create an ideal of feminine leadership as the only or best solution to today's problems. Our tenure as leaders will be more successful, I believe, if we extract gender from the equation and concentrate on those qualities and skill that work in the present circumstances and in the company of a diverse team.

My vision for leadership in the '90s, then, doesn't depend on modifiers—"female" or "Hispanic" or "African American" or any other. It does recognize and value the distinct qualities, skills and perspectives that may come from experiencing life as a member of a minority group, as well as those gained from the majority (if there is such a thing any more) or mainstream experience. This vision is built on cooperation among distinct and diverse individuals, creative solutions to complex problems and, above all, attention to the real people we serve, our students.

Leila Gonzalez-Sullivan is President of Middlesex Community-Technical College in Middletown, CT. She is a member of the American Association of Community Colleges Board of Directors and a past president of the American Association of Women in Community Colleges.

Part II

DEVELOPING WORKING RELATIONSHIPS

There are basic topics that define the presidency. Like elected officials, presidents have constituencies who require attention and without whom there is little point to what presidents do on a daily basis. In addition to constituencies we serve, other matters also demand attention: boards of various kinds to whom we are accountable; issues of financing for operating and capital needs; relationships with the media. All of these are critically important to how a president functions, how a president is perceived, and how effectively a president is able to lead the institution.

5

Constituencies

However attentive and diligent a president is, there is always a likelihood that on most days he or she will probably make someone or some constituency profoundly unhappy, while another constituency may feel deeply rewarded. There are consequences to every decision with the president's stamp on it, and even to decisions made by someone else but for whom the president takes credit or blame. It has been interesting for me to learn how the president's constituencies want to be served and how that has often differed from my illusions or expectations. The constituencies to which I am referring include faculty, staff, and students. Of course there are others, but let's look at these three groups.

FACULTY

I was a community college faculty member for five years and remember the president very well. He had been a math teacher and then an administrator for many years before opening the college in 1958 or so, and he had been president for ten or twelve years before I started teaching there. Among faculty he was legendary for appearing stern and humorless and treating us as adolescents. In fact, I was the same age as his daughter so it was no mystery to me that he didn't take me very seriously—unless he was forced to. He held monthly faculty meetings at which he took attendance, but other than that I rarely saw him. His presence was always felt, though: something slightly ominous in the background ready to pounce on any behavior which did not align with his personal code. I got a note from him once asking me why I had missed the faculty meeting the day before, and I self-righteously informed him that I had been advising a student, which I thought was "infinitely more important." That was the last "conversation" we had for about three years. But it was also the only fac-

ulty meeting I missed. I thought at the time that a little more personal contact would have been nice, and would have allowed me to see him as a
person as well as an authority figure. I also wished that he knew me as
more than that mouthy female from the English department who reminded
him of his daughter. While that never happened, I did learn some important lessons from him, some of which have helped me become a different
kind of president.

The Parent-Child Pitfall

There is something inherent in the hierarchical structure of a college
which can lead to that kind of "parent and the children" relationship between a president and the faculty. Indeed, a veteran faculty member where
I was first a president said the same thing to me one day. "You know," he
mused, "faculty are like children. They want to be noticed and praised and
made to feel good about what they do. They want to be nurtured." I knew
what he meant because I had known as a faculty member what it felt like
to be treated as a child. But it is possible to nurture without being parental;
it is possible to maintain standards and values without being authoritarian.

Faculty expect the president to put academic affairs above all else when
institutional priorities are being set. Most presidents do that. But some
presidents also protect faculty—as a parent tries to protect a child—from
institutional strains and pressures. The price that is paid for protection is
that there are faculty who don't realize the world has changed or that the
institution where they are now working for the twentieth year is not the
same as when they started. That is the parental pitfall that presidents fall
into when trying to take care of everything. We cannot treat faculty as children and shelter them from every ill wind, and then expect them to understand and act as rational adults when there are difficult choices to be made
or when priorities must change. A study done in 1985 by Earl Seidman
suggests that the reason many community college faculty said they were
disillusioned and would move into nonacademic positions if given the
chance was because not enough had been done to keep faculty involved
intellectually. Apparently we haven't been very good at engaging faculty
in the changes that have occurred in our mission and in our clientele.

We will never return to the simple days when each of us knew our
place and behaved accordingly. The institution of the future will be even
more complicated, and change will be more rapid than we dare imagine.
Faculty—and presidents—must change as well, and must not be seduced
by the myths of the past. For example, on many campuses there are schisms
between those faculty teaching primarily career-oriented programs and
courses and those who are teaching in the more traditional collegiate, trans-

fer programs. They are in separate departments, they often occupy separate facilities, and they frequently have vastly different academic and experiential backgrounds.

Since the role of the community college is increasingly a key to economic development and is the major player in job training, it seems a logical leap to then say that faculty have to overcome their differences and develop more tolerance for each other, regardless of academic background or subject matter. The focus has to be on student needs and concerns, not on which program is more legitimate because it is truly "college-level." Elitism and community colleges are, in my opinion, mutually exclusive.

Nonetheless, faculty are not the only ones who need to examine their attitudes. Presidents must make sure that institutional organizational structures and reward systems are impartial. We must make sure that all faculty voices are heard and that there are no "second-class" citizens on the faculty. Of course, there may be some institutions in which some more traditional faculty fear that they are being neglected in the rush to provide job training programs and in all the publicity that presently surrounds business partnerships and the inevitable advance of technology. It is up to the president to be even handed with all faculty and to keep the college focused on the *student*.

I have some concern that whatever conflicts do exist between presidents and faculty are exacerbated by faculty employment agreements which ultimately cater to the lowest common denominator. In their efforts to control curricular issues and guard against violation of academic freedom, most faculty associations or bargaining units have developed elaborate systems which attempt to define everything else about the position: how many hours they must be in the classroom, how many hours they must spend in their offices, how many college committees they have to join, how many advisees they must counsel, how many course preparations they must endure in any semester, when the semester or quarter may begin, when it must end, how they will be evaluated and by whom.

These are all legitimate issues with which faculty should be concerned. And the fact that presidents and deans have to think about them as well does provide some consistency and equity in the organization which makes decision-making easier in many cases. However, as educators we then spend a lot of time dealing with *minimum* standards and *minimum* expectations. Curricular decisions and scheduling of classes may be determined not by what is best for the students but by what is possible within the confines of whatever working arrangements we have with faculty. Thus, faculty have what they want: control of the academic side of the house. But at what price to the organization?

I have worked as a president in collective bargaining states which have had state-wide faculty bargaining units since 1975 or so. Many of the decisions I make as president are controlled by agreements reached to solve problems we have never had at our college though they may have existed at a college many miles away. Therefore, the relationship I have as president with my faculty is developed within contractual arrangements, often to the detriment of what we would be discussing or how we would be behaving if we were more autonomous. For example, it is difficult, if not impossible, to talk about innovations or technology or even changes in the academic calendar. If we discuss technology which could change how instruction is delivered, the discussion turns to debate about how to calculate the workload so that no one is either overworked in comparison to colleagues or underworked and therefore "getting away with something." If we want to talk about learning modules or mastery learning or changing the length of the semester or the time of day that classes are offered, the discussion again dies of its own weight because of what is possible under the terms of the contract. It so clearly spells out starting and ending dates of the semester or grading systems or what is considered a "regular" class and therefore part of the teaching load, versus an "extra" class for which one also is paid extra. It seems that our dreams about what education can or should be are stifled. The world is spinning more rapidly every day, yet we are still a hierarchical organization operating on an agrarian calendar with a funding base more appropriate for 1980, and adhering to some traditions established in the Middle Ages. What is it that faculty and presidents are supposed to talk about?

Even in colleges which are not subject to the confines of collective bargaining, there are still many intricacies to the dance between presidents and faculty, characterized by the reality that we *all* want to lead. Since most presidents have at one time been faculty members, we do know the dance from the faculty side. Furthermore, many of us promise ourselves that we will not change our steps once we "change sides". But from the other side, suddenly we are forced to see the whole dance floor, not just the part of the floor being danced on by other faculty. And once that point of view changes, the steps change as well and some of the struggle begins. Faculty want to make sure that we don't forget what it looks like from their side, and we spend our time trying to get them to learn a few new steps. As collegial as the relationship might be between a president and the faculty, there is no ignoring the differences.

Kerr and Gade (1986) maintain that faculty attitudes toward presidents are "often viscerally anti-administration or at least not pro-administration." (p. 46) Mintzberg also talks about this type of relationship in his discussion of the professional bureaucracy (1979). Professionals want to make sure that in their organizations they will be governed by other professionals just like themselves. It is very important to them to know that their "leaders" understand them and can be controlled by them because of the deference to that similarity. What they don't count on is that once a peer has been elevated in a hierarchical organization, the pressures of the organization will usually take precedence over the affiliation of the profession. The dance changes.

FACULTY AND NON-FACULTY PROFESSIONALS

Another factor which has changed the relationship between faculty and presidents is the presence of an increasing number of college professional employees who are not faculty but who are more important to the institution and its students than many faculty care to admit. Some of the senior faculty at any institution are fond of talking about the early days when the college was like a family; a few hundred students, a handful of faculty, only a couple administrative types, and an old junior high school in the middle of town for a location, for example. Now they say we have changed: we are spread out on a larger campus of multiple buildings, there are more students than one can get to know personally, and there are all these administrators and others running around who are draining resources from the only important segment of the college—academic affairs. This is a familiar chorus at most colleges and certainly a popular perception among the public and among politicians: the reason that education is failing our society is because we are wasting our resources on employees who are tangential to the learning process. All we need is that log, some students, and an enlightened professor like Mark Hopkins. Instead, we have deans running out our ears, and student activities people, and financial aid officers, and admissions directors, and career counselors, and business and industry directors, and extraneous satellite campuses which have all the same extraneous positions that have nothing to do with learning.

When I was a counselor in the late seventies, the president would invariably wander by in the early morning when the other counselor and I had just arrived in our offices, stick his head in the door and say, "Who is counseling whom?" He thought that was a very clever thing to say, but we knew that it simply revealed his underlying distrust of and contempt for the student services, "touchy-feely" types who were a drain on his budget and contributed nothing to the production of FTE. (I don't remember what he taught when he was a faculty member, but his attitude was not unusual, and probably helped contribute to the myth that to become a president, one shouldn't sink roots in the ghetto of student affairs). It is true that non-teaching positions have grown at a faster rate in higher education than have teaching positions, and it is probably also true that there are some administrative positions which will be eliminated as fiscal matters worsen.

However, many of the positions which now exist are a result of federal and state mandates requiring additional reporting, additional accountability, and additional assessment of institutional practices. Moreover, there are the demands of providing programming to an increasingly diverse and "needy" clientele. If faculty are going to be allowed to continue their concentration on teaching subject matter, then there must be someone else who is going to help students solve their economic problems, their child care problems, their substance abuse problems, their learning disability problems. This has become a very labor-intensive business and indeed is not as simple as it was thirty years ago. Everything that is impeding the educational process in the elementary and secondary schools is also affecting the community college. It is no wonder that we have seen our non-faculty professional positions double over the years. And it is no wonder that faculty are frustrated by the increasing competition for scarce resources as well as competition for the attention of the president.

In spite of the complications just mentioned, my belief still is that most faculty want to teach, they care about their students, and they want to contribute to the college in other ways. They do want a president, however, who understands what they do, who knows what it is like in the classroom, and who has a basic understanding of the pressures of their various disciplines. Finally, faculty want to be served by a president who will treat them with respect and dignity, regardless of different viewpoints or perspectives. They want someone to listen.

There is a growing consensus in higher education, however, that more attention needs to be paid to the faculty role within the entire organization. There is a growing perception that the teaching profession has grown more and more self-serving, which is leading to more "micromanagement" on the part of government agencies and more public debate about faculty workloads and concepts of tenure and evaluation. Institutional assessment is a reality because the dramatic social changes and economic hardships of the recent past have made everyone more conscious of quality and value for dollars spent. Granted, most of the debate thus far about what faculty do has occurred within the context of the research university. Nevertheless, community colleges are affected by the debate, and we are working harder to convince legislators and tax-conscious citizens that we are both providing that value for their dollars and working very hard on behalf of our students. While all of us in education would prefer to keep the legislators out of our business, that attitude may be self-defeating and may result in more regulation, not less. What we have to do instead is to lead the debate ourselves.

Presidents must work with faculty to make sure they are engaging in the practices that will lead to positive results. America is a very different place from what it was. Our priority has changed from winning the Cold War to dealing with a volatile economy in which as much as 70% of our jobs may be subject to global competition. Thus, education is by necessity required to be more applied than theoretical. As stated very well by Russell Edgerton in *Change*, the new issues in teaching are "to engage students in more intensive and effective learning communities; to shift from instructing students *about* things (covering subjects) to helping students learn *how to do* things (acquire complex abilities) and to acquire the deeper levels of knowledge we call understanding and judgment." (July/August, 1993, p. 6). Perhaps, then, the most important thing a president can do in the dance with faculty is to provide opportunities and support for the kinds of discussions that can lead to this type of fundamental change. We may have a lot to talk about, after all.

STUDENTS

The first president I worked for was walking through the student lounge area one day, and I happened to be right behind him. The lounge was a large room that one had to pass through to get from one end of the main building to the other. It was filled with furniture that invited sprawling. The president spotted a student sitting in a chair with his feet in another chair that had been pulled around to use as a foot rest. To my surprise, he walked over to the student and said, "Hey, young man, get your feet off the furniture." Furthermore, the president stood there until the student, who was very startled by the whole incident, had complied. As I walked by the student, I heard him turn to his buddies and say, "Who the hell was that guy?"

Lest we get too impressed with our own status, it is a good idea to remember that most students for whom we say we are working don't have the slightest idea who we are. Most of them, if asked, would not even be able to give the president's name without looking at a catalog or student handbook. There are always students whom we will know— the president of the student government or the valedictorian of the class whom we meet at commencement, or assorted other individuals with whom we might interact during the course of the year. We also get to know those who want to complain about something and "go straight to the top."

The best way to get acquainted with students is to visit classes, or even to teach one from time to time. Every president I know who teaches a class, myself included, says at some point in the semester that teaching that class is the major contributing factor to maintaining some sanity and having fun. In fact, it reminds us why we do the things we do, but it also keeps us humble because we realize that the number of the student lives we touch directly is minuscule.

Even though most students may not know who we are and know less what we do, they are very aware of the fact that if something goes wrong, the president is someone who is supposed to fix it. Students appear frequently at the door at the end of the spring semester when it looks as though they won't graduate for some reason which is never their fault or responsibility. As hard as it is, they must be sent away if they have not yet spoken to the faculty member they blame for their plight, or to a division chair or to the academic dean. Usually the problem is solved, and the president doesn't see them again. Since most presidents are problem solvers and action-oriented individuals, it is hard not to step in and try to immediately fix everything, especially a situation involving a student. They expect it of us; they want it of us; and we want to be able to do it.

However, that again places the president in the position of acting "parental", which is no more productive for students than it is for faculty. Students are adults and must be treated as such. They also have much to teach us. Every year I am absolutely astounded by the stories that I hear about community college students and the lives they lead off campus in addition to their on-campus, student roles. I don't think I could have worked full time, raised children, and completed a college degree all at the same time, but that is what more and more community college students are doing. College is but one of their priorities, and often not the top one. We have to compete for their attention every day. The best way we can help is to insist that our colleges provide an environment which is supportive yet academically demanding. We must ensure that they will achieve as much as they possibly can and that the education they get from us is one which will prepare them to lead the life they choose in the future.

As a faculty member I used to get discouraged sometimes because our students spent so little time with us that we rarely got to witness any change in them, or to see any tangible effect that their educations were having on their lives. In spite of emphases on outcomes assessment, on figuring out ways to objectively measure the impact that education has on students, I still believe that we have to take much on faith because the result may not be known for years. Just as it is impossible for most of us to visualize what *we* will be like in twenty or thirty years, it is similarly impossible to predict what our students will or will not do as a result of their community college experience. We can all point to our former students or graduates who have become renowned or who are in positions of leadership in our communities. But the true test of our impact on students has been less visible, less measurable, and less immediate. That does not make community colleges less important to this society, however. We must remember that statistics show that community colleges are the primary source of higher education and training for women, for minority students, and for at least one half of all students attending college. That means that as the century turns, the social attitudes, mores, and work ethic of this society will be strongly influenced by people who have attended a community college at some point in their adult lives. The average American of the last century was a white male with a fifth grade education who worked on a farm. The average American by the middle of the century was a white male who worked in a factory and had a ninth grade education. The average American now is a white female who has completed at least one year of college (Lorenzo, 1992). The average American by the next century will be a non-white female who has at least an associate's degree. Are we ready?

STAFF

Just as the composition of faculty and students has changed over the years, so has the composition of other members of a college staff. As already mentioned, life at a community college is not as simple as it used to be, and non-teaching staff numbers have increased at a far more rapid rate than have full-time faculty numbers. Thus, a president has a more complex organizational structure to keep track of and a far greater potential for conflicting priorities to monitor. But that doesn't mean that staff needs are much different from faculty and student needs. The president is still expected to be familiar with everyone's job, to see it as equally important to the institution, and to pay some personal attention to each segment of the college, if not to each individual. It is obvious that at smaller institutions with fewer employees, the president is expected to know everyone by name. The president of the larger institution will be forgiven for not knowing all six or eight hundred employees, but it is my sense in talking with presidents from all kinds and all sizes of institutions that the president who is revered and willingly followed is the one who makes an effort to get to know people, who is willing to spend time talking to people informally, and who is genuinely friendly.

It sounds easy enough, so why is it that each institution has its own set of apocryphal tales about how this or that president has no understanding of how hard people work, or has no appreciation for the complexities of life, or keeps changing the rules so that no one knows what to expect from day to day? Can it be that most presidents are really so dense? Or, is it possible that complex, hierarchical organizations are inherently dysfunctional? The adage that "where one stands on an issue depends on where one sits in the organization" has been one of the things that has helped me understand the wide variety of perceptions that exist on singular issues. It has also served as a reminder to me that communication is at best a miracle—what a president says is not always what staff hears. There are many chances for essential messages to be garbled by those who restate them as well as by those who hear them first hand.

Therefore, I have concluded that most presidents really are not as dense as many would believe, and most staff are not as deaf as presidents would believe. Staff expectations of a president are essentially the same as faculty and student expectations: someone who will talk to them; share information as well as thoughts and opinions; make an effort to understand their points of view; be fair when difficult choices have to be made; be sincere and not pretentious or judgmental; and again, someone who will honestly listen.

Defining Success for Presidents

Robert Birnbaum, in a *Trusteeship* article, stated some of these same principles in a discussion of why some presidents succeed while others fail. His conclusions are based on data which were collected and analyzed by the Institutional Leadership Project and published in 1992. Basically, Birnbaum described ten principles which distinguish exemplary presidents from average presidents and from failed presidents. He first generalized about the three presidential paths by stating that exemplary presidents are able to help their campuses renew and improve, while average presidents are able to maintain board and administrative support but lose faculty support because of their eventual inability to manage constructive change. Failed presidents either lack basic competence for the role and lose support, or they take too many actions without consultation.

The following ten principles describe characteristics or actions of successful presidents:

1. They have made a good impression in the first moments of their presidency. They have learned to "define their roles, determine the limits of their influence, and discover what works." (p.17) They have taken time to learn and listen before acting, even when immediately seeing things which need to be corrected.

2. They listen with respect and are open to influence. Most importantly, it is apparent to constituents, regardless of how the president perceives him/herself, when the president is authentically listening and therefore open to persuasion versus listening only superficially and thus prone to manipulation.

3. They work within the existing governance structures and do not try to either dramatically change them only because they may be unfamiliar, or to circumvent them for expediency.

4. They are not simple thinkers. They are able to respond appropriately to complex problems because they do not have a linear view of leadership, and they are able to contrast conflicting ideas without losing balance.

5. They do not emphasize structured bureaucratic responses to solve problems. "When institutional efficiency was seen as a goal in itself, presidents alienated others even as they attempted to influence them" (p.19).

6. They have a strong moral foundation which is communicated in the behavior they exhibit and in their ability to maintain equilibrium regardless of the events which may swirl around them.

7. They are effective when they concentrate on institutional strengths and see faculty and staff as resources rather than the source of problems to be solved and weaknesses to be corrected.

8. They encourage leadership by others throughout the institution. When leadership is shared, the college is in a better position to respond to forces prompting change and is better able to monitor institutional effectiveness. Leadership is never the act of a single individual, and the president who accepts that principle is operating from a position of strength for the entire institution.

9. They make an effort to objectively evaluate their own performances, both by actively searching for feedback and by providing ample opportunity for interaction with campus groups. In addition, they are not prone to surround themselves with supporters who insulate them from campus realities, nor are they likely to be so autocratic that accurate feedback is inhibited through fear.

10. Finally, successful presidents realize that the presidency is a role, not a career, and are prepared to leave an institution when circumstances change or when the level of support to be an effective leader is no longer strong enough to sustain the president's efforts.

The data collected by the Institutional Leadership Project indicated that perhaps one-half of all presidents fit into the average category, while one-fourth of them fail. That leaves only one-fourth seen as being exemplary, which obviously is not enough. Our challenge is to continue to increase our knowledge of leadership, to continue to examine the relationship between leadership and followership, and to continue to create organizational structures which will support and encourage effectiveness in both arenas.

Essay

PUBLIC OR PRIVATE?
by N. Patricia Yarborough

When I was in high school, it was my dream to be able to attend a particular small, private church school in West Texas. All the preparations were made. My roommate had been assigned. I knew what courses I was going to take and I was all but enrolled when, half way into my senior year in high school, my daddy announced that I would go to a state school or no school. When questioned, he responded, "Because I said so. A state school or no school." Privately, my mom told me that daddy was too embarrassed to tell me that we couldn't afford a private school. Thus began a lifetime of thinking about the differences and similarities between public and private colleges.

After I received a bachelor's degree in music from the University of North Texas (then called North Texas State University), I was completely on my own financially. When determining where I would go for a master's degree and ultimately a doctorate, never, not once, did I consider a private college or university. (Oh, the amazing power of parents.) Something about the attitude I had accepted said, "Private schools are for rich kids. You're not rich and therefore, no private school for you."

Over the years I became an outspoken supporter of public education at all levels. My experience, coupled with my political philosophy, aimed me like an arrow straight at the heart of public education. Many years later when I moved from Texas to New England, I came face to face with a whole new world of colleagues and friends, most of whom were educated at private schools. In my world of new private school acquaintances, I began to think more about the education I had received. Had my public education been as good as my acquaintance's private school education? I began to doubt.

Eventually I had the privilege of serving as president of a public community college in New England and, a few years later, I served as president of a four-year private college in the same region. For purposes of this essay I have concentrated my thinking on very broad differences and similarities between public and private colleges.

The Myth Surrounding SAT Scores

The most wonderful aspect of the open-door community colleges is that there is not the need to search for the best and the brightest. Public community colleges are much more concerned about assisting everyone who thinks he or she can be helped by a college or technical education.

The public community college is interested in working with the "whole" student and helping him or her improve every aspect of his or her lives including work and job skills. The public community college sees the relationship between the students and the community and the improvement of both. Private colleges, on the other hand—regardless of their student base—still talk about SAT scores as if they are the driving force behind both successful and unsuccessful college students. In fact, I have found that many private colleges are enrolling students with profiles exactly like community college students. The admissions staff in private colleges seem to understand the reality of competition for students. The faculty, on the other hand, will frequently be in search of the brightest and the best for their classes. Good for them. However, after a while, one begins to fear that the students are being placed in a vise between the reality of the admissions office and the hoped-for academic standards being preached by the deans of the academic divisions. I came to realize that in many private colleges, there is much fast juggling around what was said about the SAT scores of students. In the public community college, on the other hand, there is much less emphasis on entering scores and much more stress on exiting performance and ability.

Boards of Trustees

My first experience with a board of trustees was in a public community college district. Because this was my first experience, I assumed that all boards were like state-appointed boards. Wrong!

While there are many excellent and conscientious state-appointed or elected board members, one frequently finds the positions are political in nature, and members are appointed for their financial support to the governor or other state officials. Occasionally, one lucks out and gets excellent service and advice from political appointees. Far too often, however, political board members are just that, political. In a multi-campus situation, board members sometimes develop a fondness for "the college in my district." These board members become interested in getting the best for their home districts. Maybe that is understandable in some conditions. Generally, I feel a state board member should represent all the institutions in the state and not play the political game.

Political board members frequently use their election or appointment as a plum on their resume and much too often do not undertake leadership positions the way they might. Lack of attendance at college events is not uncommon and lack of attendance at special committee meetings or even board meetings can sometimes be a problem with elected or appointed board members.

Ask a public college board member to make a significant annual contribution to the institution and you will hear more excuses than you can imagine. Responses from multi-campus or state-wide board members sound something like this: "If I gave to 'X' college, I would certainly be expected to give to the other colleges in the state. " You know the outcome: generally no contribution. Even when public boards have only one college to govern, it is considered unusual for public college board members to contribute financially to their institutions.

Private college trustees, on the other hand, are usually selected by the board and membership committee of the private college board. There are no political appointees. Members' appointments are based upon their ability to give of their money, time, and expertise. For years I've heard it called "Wisdom, Wealth, and Work." The private college board members with whom I have worked, and others I have heard about, are generally truly committed to the institution and know when they are asked to serve that their pocketbooks must be open on an annual and significant basis.

Private college trustees tend to be graduates of private institutions. They tend to understand their institution and know a great deal about it. They are accustomed to providing the policies for the school as opposed to simply insuring that the state statutes are correctly administered. Private college trustees have a lot of clout and power that generally is usurped by state policy in public institutions.

Because private colleges are more dependent upon private contributions than are state institutions, boards of private schools know that they will be asked to make an annual contribution and also that they will be expected to support with their dollars any "special projects" that are approved by the school as worthy. Trustees in private colleges, in my experience, also tend to be more supportive of college functions. Because fund raising is such an integral part of the trustee's role, attendance at school functions, as well as school events, is high on their list.

In general, I have found private college trustees to be more intimately involved with their institutions than are public college trustees, more responsible for the development of policy, and more committed to significant, annual financial contributions than their counterparts in the public sector.

Tuition Differences

While still in high school I learned about the enormous differences that exist between public and private colleges. It was not, however, until I became president of a private college that I realized first-hand how those differences can detract from an important presidential agenda.

Most schools today, private or public, do not have enough financial support to allow them to do the things they know a college ought to be doing. However, the fact remains that public institutions have a distinct advantage in that boards and presidents know that the vast majority of their operating funds will be given or allotted to them by the state. Private colleges do not have that luxury. Every penny that is used for operations comes either from tuition or gifts. Some states have policies that make it possible to give money to private schools on some modest level. Many boards and presidents of private institutions want their "freedom from the state" and are not willing to accept state funds. The reality is, however, private colleges are beginning to price themselves out of the market with tuition increases just to try to make ends meet. It is a losing battle.

I believe the only way private institutions can continue to exist is to have a strong financial base that comes from a healthy endowment. Without endowments equal to at least three years of operating costs, private institutions run the risk of finding themselves in serious difficulty.

Dormitories

It is common procedure for community colleges not to own or manage residence halls (although a few do). It wasn't until I became a private college president with dormitories to fill and supervise that I first realized the great advantage the community colleges had. The primary mission of a community college is to provide a quality education to people who live at home and to give them the academics and technical skills needed to improve their lives and the welfare of the community. There generally is no demand nor necessity for community colleges to consider residential life for its students. While today's private colleges are appealing more and more to adult students, the majority of students attending private, four-year institutions are full-time, traditional college age, and ready to be away from home. Therefore, it is usual to find dormitories on the campuses of private institutions.

Until one has been responsible for students twenty-four hours a day, it is difficult to imagine the many problems that they can bring. The costs of supervision, food, security, and recreation increase dramatically, when one considers colleges with dormitories. The dating game, health, suicide, drinking, drugs, vandalism, and what to do to fill the hours in the day, evenings, and weekends, all become serious opportunities that must be carefully addressed in schools with dormitories.

Many Similarities

I have concentrated on the differences between public community colleges and private colleges because those differences are stark and obvious to those who know both kinds of institutions. There are many similarities, however, that are worth listing. The college president, whether in a public community college or a private institution, can expect the following:

Fund raising is essential. There is never enough money.

The curriculum is in need of updating. The president sees the need to move the institution into the next century by leading the way with current and up-to-date curricular offerings. The faculty generally think the curriculum is up-to-date.

Apathy abounds (according to the student and faculty union leaders).

Food service stinks (according to students).

Security is a problem (according to parents).

There is not enough scholarship money (according to the admissions staff).

Everyone wants reserved parking.

The students are the same. Whether in a public or an independent institution, the students want to be appreciated, to be taught by dedicated faculty, and to have an inner drive that makes them think they can change the world. In all schools, the students are the best part.

And in all institutions, public and private, it is both rewarding and challenging to be a college president.

N. Patricia Yarborough has served as President of the former Mattatuck Community College in Waterbury, CT and of Teiyko Post College, also in Waterbury, CT. She has worked for several major corporations and is a principal in Yarborough Associates in Middlebury, CT.

6

Boards

As much as we may want to think of ourselves as being in charge of something, and as much as we all want autonomy, the reality in public higher education is that there is always someone else to whom presidents must report or be accountable. Either there are boards of trustees governing our colleges, or there are state wide governing boards of some kind looking after us. Sometimes we get to have both.

STATE BOARDS

Governing boards are not new in education. The first one established was the New York Board of Regents which came into being in 1794. Most were created to guide the orderly growth of higher education, but they have also been expected to deal with many complicated issues, including keeping the increasing rates of expenditure in perspective, providing for budgeting equity, and avoiding excessive program duplication.

It is not surprising that there are no two states whose governing boards operate in the same manner, or are charged with the same responsibilities; each state has had to work out its structure to meet its own needs. There is also another difference between governing boards and coordinating boards. Most coordinating boards were established for the same reasons as governing boards: to help provide for the issues facing the states' institutions; review and approval of new programs; development of priorities for capital outlay, master planning, and budgetary review. According to a study done by Glenny (1977), coordinating agencies or boards were established originally because neither the governor nor the legislators could wanted to deal with the complexities of allocating money to higher education. Often the boards, whether coordinating or governing, are purely advisory in capacity, but there is one corollary which was also discovered by Glenny: in states with many legislative and executive staffs, the boards do not have much power. Conversely, in states with less structure the boards have more influence in the governing process of higher education.

There is some disagreement about whether the power of established boards is growing or diminishing, but there is no question about the problems they are facing in order to meet present conditions and challenges. Will they be able to deal with the demographic and enrollment changes and the downward spiral of their traditional "customer"? How will fiscal constraints be met? What will be done about the demand for accountability in the programs and products of higher education? How will they meet the needs of special interest groups who have been left out of the mainstream for too long and are demanding to be integrated into the system? What role will they be asked to play in the growing tensions between executive and legislative factions in their state governments, especially regarding budgetary issues? Some responses include increased reliance on the market in the face of declining enrollments, increased centralization through consolidated governing boards to respond to accountability, and strengthening of the role of the coordinating or governing agency in order to deal with budgetary issues and crises.

Since the president is the one at the institution who deals with state governing or coordinating boards and agencies the most, many of us have suggestions for what they should be doing. For example, in response to declining enrollments at baccalaureate level institutions, the concern of the boards should be with the effective use of existing facilities and with ensuring that the dollars follow where the enrollment is going— to community colleges. In many states even though community colleges are the only ones in higher education experiencing growing enrollments, they are still the last ones in line as dollars are distributed. Community colleges often have to justify every request while colleges and research universities walk off with the lion's share of appropriations. Approximately forty percent of all students enrolled in higher education institutions are in community colleges, but I doubt that there is one state board making sure that forty percent of the higher education budget is allocated to community colleges.

Once they understand our mission, boards should also take the lead in helping us to define our goals and objectives. They should determine the role and scope of all state educational institutions and arbitrate between institutions when there is disagreement. Boards might also evaluate outcomes and have some role in the process of program review.

The most important function, however, is the leadership of the board in long range planning and in providing legislators with the vitally needed long range perspective so that more efficient and effective budgeting systems may be designed. Furthermore, the planning process should be led by the boards not for the purposes of centralization and regulation but instead to allow institutions to continue to have the flexibility and independence that they need internally. Improvement in the education we offer will be achieved through better planning, budgeting, and program review, not through increased management.

Ultimately, however, all roads lead back to the budget: its size and its destination. State boards often get so side-tracked dealing with fiscal issues that the other tasks they should be spending time on are neglected. Basically, state boards need to review budgets for three reasons: to determine how much they relate to long range policy analyses, to match program development to the state's long range plans, and to study special issues. The budget is a political document in that it determines what happens on a campus, is a statement of objectives and priorities, and is a power document. There is naturally no agreement, therefore, over who should have how much control in the budgeting process or in how that control should be exercised. State government should be responsible for three things: the overall assignment of mission, the level of funding, and the access and equality of opportunity. States must also clarify that planning is within the purview of state government while implementing is the work of the boards. Within that framework, each institution must be free to develop its own answers to problems without undue interference.

The role of state boards has been debated for as long as they have been in existence, with the general consensus being that state boards should provide the foundation on which institutions can build individually. If state boards chose not to lead us into the future, the alternatives are a return to the competitive atmosphere in which all institutions become vulnerable and may lose in the long run; or increased political intervention which certainly does not contribute to the orderly progression of higher education nor to its stability; or to even more centralization than already exists, with the specter of overwhelming bureaucratization choking the very creativity that is the core of an educated society. It is up to the state board to see that autonomy and cooperation are not mutually exclusive concepts.

INSTITUTIONAL BOARDS

In a state with a governing or coordinating board, being a community college trustee can sometimes take on the aura of middle management, particularly if the state board is prone to centralization or control. If, however, real authority is vested in the local board of trustees, it can be a rewarding experience for both the trustee and the college. As with state governing boards, there is not a model that fits the majority of community colleges. There are twenty-seven states with local boards of trustees governing 600 public community colleges. In fifteen states local trustees are elected. In the other twelve states they are appointed by the governor or by the local sponsor. Four states have a mixture within the same system: some community colleges are governed by the state board and some are governed by a local board (AACC, 1993).

A statistical profile of community college board members done in 1987 showed that while academic achievements and occupations varied, 20% had bachelor's degrees and 53% had completed some level of post graduate work. Professionals comprised 41% of all board members, with another 20% employed as corporate managers, and 14% were retired. Gender and ethnic information showed that 71% were male and 29% female. Caucasians made up 90% of the membership, while 7% were African Americans, 1% were Hispanic, 1% were Asian, and less than 1% were Native American. One-third of all board members were over 50 years of age, one third were over 60, and the majority of the rest were in their forties (AACC, 1993). It is interesting to compare the trustee profile with that profile of the community college student, which shows that 58% are female and that 42% of all minorities attending higher education are enrolled in community colleges.

The method by which a trustee finds his or her way to a board of trustees has a major influence on the dynamics of the institution and how it is run. A trustee who is elected is in many cases coming to the board with a particular agenda or a particular point of view about how the college should be run. We are probably all aware of cases in which a group of people, such as a faculty or staff, or community-based organizations, have banned together, chosen a candidate, and worked to get that candidate elected to the board. Regardless of the outcome or the issues forming the basis of the election, those kinds of activities have been known from time to time to be divisive within the institution and also in the community. At worst, presidents have lost their jobs on occasion when the balance of power on a board has changed after an election. At best, presidents have faced a kind of "starting over" process while getting acclimated to new board members and learning about them as well as teaching them about community colleges in general and their institution in particular. It is not fun for a president to get caught in the middle of a power struggle on the board, and elected boards are often more volatile than appointed ones.

Board members who are appointed rather than elected are no less political in many cases, but usually they do not have a preconceived agenda prior to their appointment. Often they are graduates of the college, or community members of some standing who have had different kinds of contact with the college over the years. Some states make sure that various special interest groups are represented in the appointments, such as labor, alumni, minorities, or representatives of the communities within the college's service area. Regardless, it is still a political process that results in appointment, albeit a more subtle one than local elections.

BOARD–PRESIDENT RELATIONSHIPS

There are a few axioms that have been touted over the years regarding board-president relationships. The first is that boards make policy and presidents manage the institution. Therefore, it is imperative for the president to keep boards out of the day to day operations and keep the board focused on planning, on financing, and on providing political influence at higher levels. In order to keep boards innocent regarding the management of the college, I have known presidents who have forbidden college employees to have contact with board members. Those examples have been at colleges with elected boards and a fair amount of turmoil, so the presidents' positions should not be oversimplified on that issue. It does seem extreme, however, and is a stance which usually doesn't work anyway.

Some boards have become notorious in other communities for trying to manage the institution by either influencing or trying to control personnel appointments, or by micro-managing the budget. Thus, there is wisdom, from a president's point of view, to keeping the board out of the administration of daily activities in order for them to concentrate more attention on the matters for which we need their wisdom and perspective. One of the more frustrating boards one president says he ever had to work with was one which spent hours at every meeting pouring over budget printouts and arguing over whether or not to pay the bill for three cases of light bulbs. Yet in those same meetings they would approve multi-million dollar building projects without blinking, or approve policy changes without in-depth discussion of the ramifications. To this day he doesn't know if his frustration was because of the board or because of the type of presidential leadership which had, over the years, allowed the board to operate in this fashion. We can only hope that things have changed, or that whoever is now the president has plenty of light bulbs and no new buildings on tap.

Another axiom is that a president must continually cultivate the board. Again, there is some wisdom to the axiom, but the image of cultivation may appear to imply a superiority on the part of the president. It is true that we must continually work on providing our boards with information so that they understand educational issues in a broad context as well as in ways specific to the institution. In that sense we do cultivate board members. We shouldn't, however, cultivate to stay on the good side of board members. If we are doing our jobs well as presidents, we don't have to spend our time merely keeping in our board's good graces. We must view them not as outsiders who must be placated, but rather as partners in this enterprise. Paul Elsner, Chancellor of Maricopa Community College, made this point in an article for the *Trustee Quarterly* (1993): "Amazingly, CEOs assume board members know less than they do; they are often overlooked as a resource. Boards have eyes, ears, and intelligence that you can never possess. As a matter of fact, they have several sets of eyes and ears—all extending to your community, your colleges, and your employees." He goes on to caution us not to underestimate the wisdom of our boards, either individually or collectively, because they can save us from making serious management errors.

Another axiom often taught is that the president should never let the board argue in public at meetings. All issues should be settled ahead of time so that a united front is presented to the public and so that, presumably, the president's authority and wisdom are not questioned. Many presidents, however, have some trouble with this particular concept even while agreeing that it is very uncomfortable for a president to watch the board publicly "discuss" an issue on which a recommendation has been made. Instead, one can believe that there are times when open discussion is healthy and that we as presidents need not live in fear of boards disagreeing on some things. To me that says we are doing our jobs by providing them with sufficient information so that they do not feel compelled to blindly accept any recommendation the president makes. When there is never any discussion or disagreement, then the opposite of the intended result can occur: members of the college community or the public feel that everything happens behind closed doors, which leads to the fear that we are hiding something from them. The important thing for presidents to remember is that just because we have the title doesn't mean we have the answers or the right to try to control every situation. In fact, the more we sometimes try to control outcomes, the more they can get away from us because we haven't listened, and we haven't given others credit for having good ideas. I have heard of presidents who took some pride in working with boards who were of divided opinion on most issues, including the issue of whether or not the president should continue working there. It was described by one president as a challenge to always make sure that he had a majority, even if by just one vote. He apparently took pleasure in "winning" and therefore manipulated the board in order constantly to set up situations in which his views would prevail—but only after much discussion and negotiation. Perhaps that situation made the president feel needed, or perhaps everything in life was a game to be won regardless of the cost. I do not think the majority of presidents would recommend that kind of "living on the edge," however. There aren't many things more destructive, over the long run, to an institution than a board of trustees in constant turmoil. When a board is unable to help set priorities for the institution because personal issues take over their thinking, then it is impossible for the president to provide true educational leadership for the college.

Yet another axiom is that board members do not like to be surprised. Neither do presidents, so we ought to understand this concept without much difficulty. Paul Elsner says, "It has been my experience that most boards will follow the lead of the CEOs, accepting even the most difficult personnel or budget recommendations, if they are properly forewarned. Unfortunately, CEOs often allow crushing, impending events to converge on them. This situation requires them to suggest a recommendation without proper briefing of the board. The board is put in the position of having to 'act now,' a disconcerting situation at best for most board members." (p.12) If we do not underestimate our boards, if we do not fear our boards, and if we remember how we wish to be treated by those who report to us, then the surprises should be very few and relatively minor to the overall functioning of the college. Of course, we cannot always predict what is going to become an issue for individual board members, but boards will remain supportive of a president if such incidents are rare.

There really is no mystery to working with boards. Basically it comes down to making sure that we take the time to treat our boards with the respect with which we also wish to be treated. We can learn much from our board members, even the ones with whom we may not see eye-to-eye, or with whom we have other personal differences.

Even as the last few years have been very hard on presidents and other employees at our colleges, they have been equally hard on boards of trustees. We have all seen our optimism diminish as we have presided over the decimation of our budgets, and board members have been directly in the line of fire for making tough decisions, just as presidents have been. Boards sometimes get criticized for supporting recommendations that we make to them, particularly if those recommendations include making some fundamental changes in how the college operates or in who will be employed there in the future. One concern I have for the future is that the best people in our communities will not be willing to serve if appointed, or to run for election if asked because of the difficulties we have had, and will be facing. The prestige of being a board member has been more than offset by the demands of the position. It is up to us as presidents to make sure that our boards are committed to working hard on our behalf, and to continue to convince potential candidates for our boards that the rewards are worth the increasing amount of public scrutiny they may have to face.

Essay

THE PRESIDENT AND THE COMMUNITY COLLEGE BOARD
by B. A. Barringer

A positive relationship between the president and the board of trustees is essential to the success of a college in fulfilling its mission. While it may be impossible to generalize about boards of trustees, certain observations may be put forward regarding what constitutes an effective or an ineffective board.

After 28 years as a community college president, having served a dozen boards and more than a hundred individual trustees, I am happy to say that, for the most part, those who serve as trustees are people with commitment to our mission and integrity of purpose. Many of our trustees have brought distinguished reputations to their roles as college advocates. There are some, of course, who take more from a college than they give; these, luckily, are in the distinct minority.

In my many years of service, I can recall only a few trustees whom I would describe as actually being destructive to the life and fabric of the college. While few in number, these individuals shared a number of common characteristics:

- They possess inflated egos

- They work as individuals rather than as members of a team

- They ask the administration for special favors

- They tend to be deficient in their professional lives

- They are powerless people within the other domains of their lives; they see their role as trustee as a sole source of power

- They are petty, selfish and unforgiving

- They trust no one

- They ask the administration for inordinate amounts of information

- They are overly concerned with personnel matters: who is hired and fired

- Each action tends to be personal and undertaken with little regard for establishing or confirming goals and policies

- They violate rules of confidentiality

- They are often found on campus gathering evidence and entertaining complaints about the administration

- They tend to allow themselves to be placed on the board to carry out a specific agenda for some group or constituency; i.e., political, ethnic, economic, or union

At the other end of the spectrum are the trustees who are successful and whose tenure on the board benefits the college. This group shares these common characteristics:

- They bring distinguished records of public service to the board

- They don't ask for personal favors from the administration

- They are conscious of and act on the proposition that power emanates from the board as a whole, not from individual activities

- They understand the board's primary role is policy development

- They are knowledgeable about the college

- They are generally supportive of the administration but will differ and raise questions when they are not convinced of the efficacy of a particular action taken by the administration

- They tend not to have hidden agendas

- They tend not to represent specific groups; they think more broadly and inclusively. They understand that their role on a public board is to represent the public

- They tend to be more trusting of the administration's actions (a trust that has been developed and earned)

- Although most are appointed or elected in a partisan environment, their actions reflect their own personal feelings rather than being an echo of a particular political faction

- They, too, can be found on campus frequently; they will listen to

staff concerns, but make no commitments or promises, and will
share these concerns with the president

The crucial element in board/president relations is trust; without it,
little can be accomplished. In fact when trust disappears, the board is
often drawn into the role of administering the daily activities of the
college, and while this is inappropriate behavior, it is understandable.
Board members feel vulnerable when they do not trust their president
because they are, after all, liable for the institution. So they begin to take
actions to keep themselves out of jeopardy.

I once served as interim president at a community college where
trust between the former president and the board had disintegrated.
When I arrived at the college, I found individual board members were on
campus daily, giving directions to various staff officers, removing
personnel files of individual faculty members from the college to their
homes, and convening a finance committee of three—a committee that
heard individual salary appeals and granted salary relief to some individuals and not to others. The result of all of this was that 59 grievances
had been filed against the college. Unfortunate as this situation was, I
recognized that this trustee "administrative activism" grew out of the
board's loss of confidence in their chief executive officer.

I believe it is logical to assume that the board wants the president to
succeed, if for no other reason than because the trustees are the ones who
hired him or her. In reality, it takes much to cause a board to become
disenchanted with institutional leadership. Many boards are reluctant to
read the signs and symptoms of emerging problems with their CEO until
the situation is beyond salvaging. In fact, boards are sometimes the last
to know or admit that their administrative leadership is failing.

While the word "evaluation" can connote a number of negative
images, regular board evaluations of the president can very positively
affect the tenure of each. Unfortunately, many boards give little or no
constructive feedback to their president. If there is no evaluation of her/
him, they must wait until something goes wrong before they take action.
As interim president, I have replaced a number of presidents who have
been terminated. In many cases, these presidents indicate that they had
no real awareness of the board's feelings.

I have worked with boards that are divided into factions, with each
faction representing a special interest. There is nothing wrong with
board members disagreeing over issues and there is nothing wrong with
a split vote in a board meeting—as long as that vote is not motivated by
political or personal issues but, rather, reflect a substantial philosophical

difference on a particular issue. It is particularly dangerous when the split vote is *always* along the factional lines, regardless of the issue. When faced with a divided board, the administration must treat all board members equally and try to find a common denominator: that which is good for all *students*. The administration cannot succumb to any one faction of the board.

The board chair is a crucial position and, as the first among equals along with his or her substantial appointing authority and agenda control, can facilitate successful board actions. Because the president will have the greatest contact with the board chair, the relationship between these two individuals will, in turn, affect the entire board.

The president and the chairperson must understand one another and be able to assist each other at the appropriate times. There is substantial power inherent in most board chair positions and, very often, great wisdom and maturity is demanded to carry out the duties of the chair. Unfortunately for many boards, there are chairs who do not possess these characteristics, and their boards are far less effective because of it.

Probably the most ineffective board chair I ever served took great advantage of her position and made unilateral decisions with which other board members disagreed. Surprisingly, while very upset with the chair, the other board members refused to attempt to unseat her or remove her from her very powerful position. In my experience, a situation within a board must be absolutely intolerable for other board members before they attempt to purge one of their fellow members. Often, it is the CEO who pays the price for ineffective board leadership.

A board chair once directed me to fire a particular staff member. Having just arrived at the college to serve as interim president, I asked the reason. He replied that this staff member went home for the day every day at noon. How, I asked, did the board chair happen to have this information? He told me that he had been following this staff member every day! This is obviously not a trustee whose own work kept him busy.

My own investigation into the matter indicated that the staff member was under-employed at the college, through no fault of his own. He was willing to accept additional work at no increase to his salary, and did so successfully.

This same board chair single-handedly nearly destroyed his college's contract negotiations. After difficult negotiations, the college reached tentative conditions of the contract, which were approved by the board in executive session. Immediately thereafter, the board chair attended a conference for the Association of Community College Trustees. Proving that "a little knowledge is a dangerous thing," he called me from the conference and directed that I stop all negotiations, based on something he heard at the seminar.

I did as directed by the board chair. The result was a two-day strike and, eventually, a settlement which was the same as had been proposed and agreed upon earlier.

This kind of activity puts the president in a very difficult position: being asked to carry out a directive from the chair means the president must take actions that may be tempered—or even reversed—at a later time by the entire board. At best, the president is in an uncomfortable position with the rest of the board. At worst, he or she will be held accountable for the results of the chair's directive.

Over the years, I have witnessed instances where there is no confidentiality among certain board members, even in sensitive personnel issues. Certain members may attempt to gain special access to information which gives these individuals the power of knowledge. The recourse to this phenomenon is for the president to insure that every board member receives the same information. At the very least, other board members should be told that one of their colleagues has been the recipient of special information.

There are boards and administrators who measure their commitment to their institutions by the length of board meetings. This is the board who meets for endless hours, when much of the effectiveness of their actions wanes after the first two. There are rare exceptions that require longer meetings, but meeting length and board effectiveness should never be confused.

Some boards need to understand that their primary and formal contact with the college is with the president. If there is unhappiness among board members with any actions or reports of the president's staff, it is inappropriate behavior for board members to chastise the staff either in public or private. Rather, they should communicate to the president their lack of satisfaction. Of course, there are those presidents who, rather cowardly, allow their staff to take blame from the board, and this is wrong also.

Almost all boards with which I have worked can articulate a reasonable definition of their role as policy makers who hold the administration responsible for implementation. The problem is that some boards understand this principle only in the theoretical sense; translating it into action is more difficult. Do not assume that the board can or will make the connection from theory to practice simply because they can articulate the principle. This is the reason that boards as well as presidents need regular in-service education to continually analyze what they are doing and why.

In my many years in the president's office, I have worked with many dedicated trustees whose primary concerns were the college and its mission. I have also worked with some who have contributed very little to the effectiveness of the organization and a few have actually been destructive. Then there were the trustees who made my work more "interesting:" the trustee who carried a pistol in his boot; the trustee whose main objective when attending any out-of-town conference was to find the nearest massage parlor; the trustee whose sole purpose was to ensure that her friends were given jobs at the college and who called the president (and human resources director) every day with that message; the trustee who held nothing in confidence, including the board's collective bargaining plans; the trustee who wanted the presidency for himself and who drove the president out so the office would be conveniently vacated; and those who were impervious to the wails and trauma on the campus because it was too much trouble to ensure that the president carry out the mission in a positive way.

Anyone who has been a president for any length of time can probably add a few examples to this list. But it is my opinion that the community college board is one of the strongest mechanisms in the governance of higher education. I know of no group who can number among their members more people who are genuinely committed to students and to what we are attempting to do in this great community college movement.

B. A. Barringer has served as President and Interim President of numerous institutions, including ten years at Catonsville Community College in Maryland and Brookdale Community College in New Jersey. Barringer is the principal of Gold Hill Associates in Gold Hill, NC.

7

Financial Issues

HISTORICAL PERSPECTIVE

Most community college presidents have had to guide an institution through at least one period of recession or decline in financial support. And, except for those of us who became presidents recently, almost every community college president also has been able to guide an institution through periods of financial health and growth. But it appears now that periods of unfettered fiscal growth for public education will not recur and that we will be doing well to claw back to some level of parity with inflation.

Until the 1950s when state support became more common, community colleges were often totally supported by local districts. The community college was in fact developed as a particular type of educational institution with commitments to democratize higher education and to serve local constituents. As we have grown, however, so have the problems associated with our financial support.

Five sources of support have traditionally formed the financial basis of the community college: local taxes, state taxes, federal taxes, gifts and grants, and student tuition and fees. In many states, there has been a partnership between the local and state governments to provide at least two-thirds of the funding necessary, with the final third supplied by charges to students and by gifts and grants. Over the past ten to twenty years, however, it has been increasingly necessary to shift from local to state support: the increased demands of higher enrollments have not been able to be met by the limitations of local resources; the small geographical size of local districts which was supposed to mean equal access really has not insured that equality; and community colleges have had to face the same equity controversies as

the public schools— should residents of wealthy districts have better educational systems than those in poorer districts?

Since the community college origin was rather hybrid in nature, growing both out of the elementary/secondary mode and also out of the higher
education mode, it should not be surprising that community college financing mechanisms have been a reflection of those used in both other
sectors of education. The original purpose of the junior college as conceived
by William Rainey Harper was to relieve higher education institutions of
the burden of providing the general, less specialized education of the first
two years of college. At this point in our history, it seems particularly ironic
that Harper, who had such an influence on the development of the junior
college, also was the pioneer in changing the face of the American university from one which taught and prepared students for a better economic
future to an institution which concentrated on "investigation" and made it
clear that results and publications would determine salaries and other faculty benefits. If Harper had not had the dream of establishing a different
kind of American research university back in 1892, then the junior college
might not have evolved, either.

Thus, the idea of extending the responsibility of the public schools for
two more years so that resources available to higher education could be
used more efficiently in the direct preparation of students for graduate
school was the basis of the local financial support of the junior college
(Brenneman and Nelson, 1981). Generally speaking, however, the financing pattern for community colleges changed significantly between the early
part of the century and 1970, with a reduction in reliance on local funding
coupled with an increase in state funding as well as the commonplace use
of tuition and fees.

In the 1970s, new problems relating to the financing of community colleges emerged as we continued to expand. The problems essentially were
caused by an unanticipated demand for community college education, the
shift from full-time to part-time students, the unavailability of funds, and
an unwillingness to limit access by raising tuition and fee levels in the face
of declining local and state support. Even now, some of these issues have
not been resolved. The financing of community colleges has lagged behind
the mission of serving more diverse clientele pursuing more diverse objectives. Our continued growth in enrollments even while resources have been
diminishing has, some believe, eroded our credibility. It is essential that
we discuss the relationship between institutional aspiration and available
resources as we work to minimize these problems.

Most of us have horror stories to share about financial shortfalls, or
budget reversions that have been mandated in the middle of the fiscal year.
The latest generation of fiscal flu started in the Northeast, rippled less se-

verely through the Midwest and has come to the West Coast with a re-
sounding force. Regardless of the details, we are experiencing variations
on the same theme: financial support for public higher education has become theoretical. The public demands excellence with no price tag.

In addition, K-12 public education is in the same bind. In fact, America's
educational policies continue to heap more and more social responsibility
on the schools without the corresponding increases in financial support.
The public schools are expected to deliver students who can read, write,
and think, yet they are expected to do it in the face of overwhelming odds
against reading and writing and thinking: hunger, neglect at home, abuse,
fear, violence, MTV, and hormones that start raging at a younger and
younger age because of all that children see, hear, and experience on the
streets—urban and suburban. Meanwhile, budgets continue to deterio-
rate as problems mitigating against education escalate.

The demographic changes in this country are one part of the dilemma;
in some states, for instance, only 21% of the tax paying population has
children in school at *any* level. To expect over three-fourths of the public to
pay more for a service they do not use any more (at least in their minds) is
a recipe for continued defeat. In addition, the perception among the public
(and those elected to public office) that there is bureaucratic bloat raging
on our campuses does not help make our case. It is very difficult for people
to see a connection between quality of life and level of educational attain-
ment. The statistics are there to show that a community college graduate
will earn 58% more taxable income than a high school graduate and 320%
more than a high school drop-out (Department of Commerce, Bureau of
Census Current Populations Report, 1990). But there are no hard statistics
to talk about the connection between education and other quality of life
issues. Educators firmly believe that there is a connection—that investing
in education may mean less investing in prisons and social welfare programs because people who are educated are more able to take care of themselves and to cope with daily life. But the general public is saying "Show
me." And we cannot. Therefore, our pleas for more money are seen as ar-
guments only to line the pockets of administrators who are already over-
paid and to pay teachers more for working less. After all, who in the business world gets to work only nine months of the year and only six hours
per day? As they say, the three best things about teaching are June, July,
and August. Senior citizens on fixed incomes with no children in school
are unwilling to pay higher taxes; people who are unemployed or in fear of
soon becoming unemployed are unwilling to pay higher taxes; those on
welfare with children cannot pay anything; the rich can afford to send their
children to private schools and therefore have little concern for public education; and many middle class families with *or* without children are get-

ting hammered on all sides by taxes and fees. At the end of this century it is very difficult to justify additional spending on school systems that are merely the reflections of a society which many believe is itself in serious disarray. It is discouraging, and difficult to keep in perspective.

Facing a Difficult Future

Choosing to become, or remain, a community college president means that for the foreseeable future, budget and financial discussions will dominate everything we do, every decision we make, and every argument in which we engage about those decisions. Budgets are the symbols of our priorities, and the process by which we choose and achieve those priorities is the key to our institutional survival.

The times facing us are not for the faint of heart. Fiscal and financial obstacles have to be seen as people and ethical issues. The crunching of numbers is far less of an obstacle than the impact of our decisions on the people at our institutions and in our communities.

First of all, we have to have general institutional agreement on our mission. It is even more important in lean times to reach consensus on institutional purpose and for obvious reasons: competition for scarce resources can destroy an organization if there is no underlying belief that all of the competitors want basically the same things in the long run. It is up to the president to force discussions about mission to occur regularly, even when the groans of, "Not this again" echo through the halls. And it is up to the president to listen to what people are saying and to bring that information to bear on budgeting decisions.

Agreement on mission can then lead to a strategic planning process that gets things in some order of priority. As stated by Kay McClenney, Vice President for the Education Commission of the States, "You have to know what you are going to do without." A strategic plan can serve as a catalyst for making some otherwise impossible choices. We used a process several years ago when things were at their worst in the state, and we were being told to cut our budgets on a monthly basis. Our Planning and Finance Committee, composed of elected members from every segment of the college, was told to develop a list of ten elements of the college which reflected what we do and who we serve. They were then told to list them in descending order of priority so that any cuts that were made at that point would be from the bottom of the list up. As one might imagine, things were very serious at this point. We had already jettisoned everything we could from the operating budget, had laid off all part-time employees as well as eight managers, one clerical staff, and eight faculty. I was also at that time considering contracting out cleaning and security functions, which would result in the lay-offs of another fifteen people. We had raised student charges fairly dramatically in the previous two years, so we couldn't look there for additional revenue. The committee did its work and presented a list of ten strategic priorities, knowing that if further reductions occurred, I would go to their list and work my way to the top until the budget was balanced. It was an excruciating time for all of us.

I only had to act on the last three items on the list, but without that process there would have been even more distrust than already existed due to the unprecedented steps that had been taken or recommended regarding personnel. I also learned a valuable lesson: while there must be involvement in difficult decision-making, when choices ultimately do affect personnel, the president is the only one who can be involved in the end. Thus, another dichotomy is created. On the one hand, the president must encourage participation; on the other, she must become dictatorial.

Luckily the institution has not faced the same level of severity in its funding crunch since that time. But neither has it totally rebounded from those days, and I don't know if it ever will. We now deal with the reality of institutions not having enough money on which to operate even adequately coupled with the declining morale of our employees. These times bring out the worst in all of us: the competition, judgmental and critical tendencies, defensiveness, and high stress levels. People are working harder and feeling less appreciated. And they are fearful of being on the next list of those targeted for lay-off, which increases the stress levels and causes more conflict and competition. All the talk among corporate leaders and politicians about being "leaner and meaner" plays well to consumers and taxpayers, but it wreaks havoc within the organization. We need to figure out ways to be leaner without becoming meaner or we will be like the tiger chasing its tail until we self-destruct.

In addition to keeping the institution focused on its mission and long-term health, and insisting on a level of involvement in decision-making, the president must do two other things as well. Since the president is the one person in the organization with the most comprehensive information on which any financial decisions are made, it is incumbent upon him to share that information with others. When there is a perception that something is being hidden or manipulated behind closed doors, then everyone in the organization becomes suspicious of everyone else. As stated earlier, tight times bring out the worst in all of us, so the president has to try continually to minimize negative behavior or negative perception by being truthful, by providing opportunities for others to ask questions, and by answering those questions honestly.

The second thing a president must do is to appear confident, reasonable, and optimistic to a certain degree. These elements of a president's demeanor are not intended to hide or cover up the truth, but to help keep anxiety down. So now is the time to listen, to be patient to the point of biting the tongue, and to toughen the hide. Good problem solving does not occur in a group which is on the verge of panic or which does not have accurate and timely information. In the end, most people do not want to make fiscal decisions; they want the president to do it. But they *do* want to have their opinions and concerns heard and acknowledged.

I have always tried to remind myself and others that even as bad as times have been, it could have been worse. We must learn from the adversity we have experienced, make the hardest decisions first, and then build on the strengths that remain. Donald Rippey, a former community college president and recently retired professor of higher education at the University of Texas once said about making tough decisions, "If you have to swallow a toad, don't just sit there and look at it. Swallow it." I didn't really understand that quaint "Texas talk" until facing my first real fiscal crisis as a president. His is simple advice. It is also good advice, and like most, easier to look at than to swallow.

EMERGING FROM CRISIS

Coming out of a fiscal crisis is no picnic either. There is great potential danger if we are not careful about how we manage or lead an institution after the crisis has passed and we are left with picking up the remaining pieces. When the pressure has eased, the politicians have finished ranting and raving and doing monthly purges of the allocations, and students have continued to enroll in spite of increased costs, the institution enters a kind of twilight zone: we spend a year or two on a maintenance program in which we are able to meet basic costs and obligations and do not have to take more away from anyone. Then, we get back into more dangerous territory if we get to a place where discretionary spending is again possible, even at the smallest level.

After several years of perceived deprivation, everyone is ready to have his or her priorities put first on the list. Faculty see the possibility of hiring some full-time instructors that are "desperately" needed; everyone wants more funding for travel and professional development; the physical plant staff usually have lists a yard long about all the repairs and renovations they want to make; the computer labs need upgrading. The lists are endless. The problem is that since there still is not enough funding to meet everyone's needs, the cycle of competition and the "jockeying for position" continues almost more intensely than when cutbacks were being made.

It should be no surprise that it is harder to manage the emergence from crisis than it is to manage the plunge into it. When everyone in the organization is made to feel that the sacrifice is equal, that all are contributing to survival, then those same people will endure hardship for a surprisingly long time. They may not like it, but they will tolerate the circumstances. Our priority as presidents, now and in the future, is to make sure that no one feels more deprived than anyone else but that all understand the concept of "priorities" and "taking turns." We must look at organizational structure, at how decisions are made, and at how information is circulated within our organizations in order to maintain the communication so necessary. Just as binge and purge cycles are deathly in individuals, they are deathly to organizations. The temptation is to reward ourselves for being such good campers when things were tough by splurging on something—"just this once." However, we cannot afford the splurge, in whatever form, because the gap between what we need and what we have available is not going to lessen.

One element which is important in any discussion of budgeting, either at the campus or at the governmental level, is the element of equity. Equity is not as important in good times, but when resources are scarce, equity becomes the slogan for all who feel left out or slighted or less influential in the budgeting process. Some writers have noted that the university organization is like other bureaucracies in that the roles of power and bureaucratic rules in budgeting change when resources are scarce: rules become less apparent than power (Hills and Mahoney, 1978). Thus, budgeting systems have to be designed so that they counteract political behavior associated with gaining power and result in equity and efficiency.

FORMULAS

The most common route to achieving equity and efficiency that has been taken, both in legislative bodies and in campus budgeting processes, has been via a formula of some kind. Formulas mean many different things: they are aids to calculations which reduce complexity; they outline assumptions on the function of the institution; they help establish priorities and set standards of institutional operation; they serve as guidelines for future budget discussions, and they often provide an element of stability and control. Budgeting formulas are typically adopted in order to reduce political uncertainties and to improve equity. In addition, formulas can provide a basis for greater accountability, which is becoming increasingly important with regard to the use of tax dollars.

Formulas also have dysfunctions, however. First of all, they do not always recognize quality. Secondly, they sometimes provide a twisted image of reality based on the sociological principle that whenever phenomena are simplified from the complex, much information is compacted and therefore lost. The result is a kind of distortion based on incomplete information. Third, there is usually a difference between costing and pricing, meaning that formulas may accurately reflect the price of some activities, but too often they do not allow for complete support of the cost of those activities. Finally, formulas accent the tension between the need for stability in the funding process and the desire for flexibility that is every manager's mantra.

Most states rely on some kind of formula for deciding the level of funding support for community colleges, and although there is fairly general agreement that the use of formulas in the budgeting process is not totally negative, there is little agreement on the formula model that should be used. In spite of that, probably the most common state aid formula that is employed is based on the number of full-time equivalent student enrolled, or projected to be enrolled. Even those states without a formula of some kind are moving rapidly into the formula funding arena as a response to the turbulent times. Taxpayers and elected officials want to know how their money is being spent, and those responsible for dividing up the pie into smaller and smaller chunks are desperately searching for an objective way to approach their increased poverty.

Formulas have their usefulness on campuses as well, for the same reasons as they are employed by local and state governments. Objectivity, equity, and efficiency in the budgeting process serve us well and make our jobs as presidents a bit easier when money is hard to find. There are some advantages to not having much discretionary spending to do—or to justify to those who disagree with our choices. Allocation formulas are helpful if 1) we have agreed on our mission and 2) we have agreed on institutional priorities. They also can serve as a basis for assessment from year to year, particularly if we are willing to adjust them pending the assessment results.

CAPITAL FUNDING ISSUES

Another problem area in the financing of community colleges has been capital funding for buildings and maintenance of existing facilities. In the beginning, many junior colleges moved in with their secondary school mentors, and some community colleges still occupy abandoned public school facilities. Others have set up their operations in old commercial buildings which have been purchased or donated to the cause. Some have established elaborate physical plants which occupy acres of land and often branch out to other locations in their service areas. (One of our faculty on sabbatical several years ago visited many campuses similar to ours in towns of similar size in the East and Midwest. Her conclusion was that it seemed that all community colleges were built on a parcel of land on a slight hill on the edge of town. I had to laugh because five of the six colleges where I have worked fit that description perfectly.)

There are many patterns to describe our physical plants, however, and there are also community colleges with no recognizable campus at all. What is common to those with physical plants include an expectation, in colleges with a local funding base, that funding for capital projects will be local, either through local government outlay, bonding, or serious fundraising. Thus it is not surprising that even in 1980, a study by Howard Bowen discovered certain patterns for community colleges that were a reflection of the affluence of the local area. He found a direct correlation between the relative wealth of the community college district and the size of the physical plant, which seems to be a result of the expectation that local districts will provide money for facilities. Imagine the headaches for those in states with no local funding base but with total dependence on the state for capital as well as operating budgets. The attitude seems to be for us that if we didn't get what we wanted in the initial construction phase, even if that was over twenty years ago, then we are just out of luck.

Meanwhile, maintenance has been deferred to the point that billions of dollars are needed nationally for the upkeep and repair of present facilities, not to mention mandated changes required by the Americans With Disabilities Act. Bowen's findings have been supported over the years in studies by NACUBO, by various state education agencies, by the Education Commission of the States, and more importantly by the experiences we have all had on our campuses with trying to find the money to make necessary renovations as well as emergency repairs.

The problems we are facing are obvious: growing enrollments have made space for classrooms and labs as well as for offices a hotly-contested issue on many campuses; designs of the 60s and 70s when most new campuses were being built do not especially reflect the needs of the 90s and beyond; and operating budgets which have not even kept up with inflation have made it difficult—if not impossible—for presidents to choose "buildings over people and supplies" when making fiscal decisions. Throw in a few fires, hurricanes, floods, or major blizzards, and we get a brew that is interesting when not fatal. And I haven't even mentioned the issue of parking spaces.

As is the case with most problems, identifying them is easier than knowing what to do about them. The president must again walk a very tight rope in order to do what is best for the institution in the long run and satisfy immediate desires for the short run. Once again the college where I was first a president is a good example of the problems we face. The campus is now twenty years old and aging rapidly. It was designed by an architect from California who understood little about New England weather, and was built by a state which was cutting corners then as well as now. As a result there have been some major problems over the years with roofs leaking (they are flat), with walls leaking (the waterproofing of the concrete was the first item to fall under the budget ax during construction). It is built on the side of a hill (a nightmare for anyone on crutches or with other mobility issues), the boiler which heats the plant is on the down slope, which means that steam has to be pumped uphill (utility bills are always interesting, since cold prevails for at least half of every year), and the wiring is underground (allowing ground water, which cannot go anywhere because of the rock ledge on which the campus sits, to methodically corrode wires and pipes). Needless to say, that campus has had its share of problems, emergency repairs that took the state five years to fund, and other assorted dilemmas regarding accessibility and energy usage. Had more foresight gone into the planning of the campus, they might be spending less now on repairing things and worrying much less about when the next emergency is going to be.

When our complaints are added to those of every other state agency, however, they do not seem so critical to lawmakers who control the appropriations. At every level of government there has been an unwillingness to allocate funds for future needs; thus, the last item in a budget to receive any attention is the one labeled "Repair". (Even Yale, whose annual operating budget is at least $200 million more than some states spend on their entire higher education system, has a deferred maintenance problem.)

As difficult as it is, the president and governing boards have to start insisting that a certain portion of an institution's income be designated for capital projects. If we continue to rely on either local or state governments to fund capital projects in addition to other expenditures, then we will not only postpone, but also exacerbate it.

In addition, most institutions have been driven by a budget process that has required all funds to be expended in one fiscal period. Thus, rather than being able to set funds aside and use them later, we have been forced to "spend it or lose it" and have therefore chosen to spend budgets on immediate needs. Purchasing of expensive equipment or building up accounts in order to afford major construction or renovation projects has been almost impossible in the last few years. The very attributes that we encourage in individuals— saving money for a later date to support retirements or college educations for our children, for example—are discouraged within institutions because of the political systems in which we have to operate.

The classic double bind from which we may never recover is that on the one hand, if we don't spend all of our allocations, they are taken away from us; on the other hand, if we try to save money from income earned rather than money allocated, then there is a suspicion that someone or something is being shortchanged. Legislators are suspicious of institutions with reserve accounts but will decry a president's management skills if an institution has no reserve.

The same kind of bind is evident on many campuses as well. When times are tight, institutions have had to spend more from reserves to supplement inadequate appropriations—just in order to keep the college doors open. We have made commitments to our students and to our employees and have been very creative about how we have met our obligations to both groups. While it is commendable, it also has been partially self-destructive because we have failed to convince either the public or the various governments that we are underfunded, especially when we are compared to the overcrowded prisons and courts or to mental hospitals and nursing homes. There simply is no contest. Education loses every time.

There is a point, however, when an institution must decide that it will not spend its reserves to below a certain level. The president must be the guardian of that level and make sure that it is maintained. The problem occurs when, in the most difficult of circumstances, there must be layoffs of personnel in order to meet an operating budget and there is money in reserve accounts which the president must refuse to spend. How do you explain to someone who just lost his job that, yes, this college has maybe a million dollars at its disposal for an emergency, but it cannot continue to fund a $20,000 or $30,000 salary? To the person affected there *is* no greater emergency, and a president who must take a stand contrary to that individual's needs must certainly have lost touch with human compassion. And when, a year or two later, that same president makes a decision that a certain part of the physical plant is useless at a variety of levels and must be repaired or redesigned, the person who lost his job and his friends who remain will be the last ones to understand institutional priorities.

The situation just described may be extreme, but the assumptions are not: the major reason that we have such an enormous problem right now with our plants falling apart is that we have almost always chosen to invest in people rather than in buildings. We have also been forced to manage our funds inefficiently because of the nature of the political process and the desire of those who dole out the money to control how it is spent. And now that we are at an absolute crossroads in the financing of government at all levels, the choice to maintain physical plants and create long range plans, possibly at the expense of personnel or immediate desires, is going to be the single most important and difficult issue that presidents will have to face.

Thus, we have at least two tasks ahead of us regarding capital funding. One is to work on bringing more rationality into the budgeting process at the legislative level, and another is to continually educate our constituents about budget and planning processes and how choices get made. Human nature being what it is, the president must not expect that everyone will understand saying "no" to personnel requests while saying "yes" to physical plant renovations. But given the prognosis for the immediate future, we will have to continue to make those kinds of hard choices. It is what makes us wake up in the night wondering sometimes if what we are doing is right or fair or logical.

Essay

THE VICISSITUDES OF YEAR ONE
by Dorothy Franke

Some people have asked me if I would have taken this job if I knew beforehand the problems that would confront my new presidency. As I write this, I am unsure. Perhaps the telling will decide.

Kirtland Community College is small (fifteen hundred credit students a semester), rural (no town larger than six thousand in a district of 2500 square miles of pines, rivers and lakes) and poor (the counties served by Kirtland have the lowest per capita income in the lower peninsula). Aside from services to the inhabitants and a paper mill, tourism is about the only business in the area. The college sits at the junction of the four major counties it serves, on 160 acres of land so beautiful it makes your throat ache.

The college is funded by tuition, a state allocation, and a local property tax called a millage. A millage can only be levied by a vote of the college's constituents. Kirtland began with a charter one mill when the college was voted into existence in 1965. Twenty-five years later, in 1990, it was still operating on one mill, having failed in seven elections over the years to get more operating money from the local citizens. State aid was becoming tighter. The only source of income the college had any control over was tuition. It had risen from $20 to $40 per credit hour from 1985 to 1990.

To add to the bleak financial picture, the college also found itself in a major academic scandal. The former president of Kirtland had decided to retire in June, 1990. It was assumed his successor would be the college's vice president, a young, dynamic educational leader who had worked his way up the ladder from grant writer to vice president. His rise was accompanied by master's and specialist's degrees, and finally a Ph.D. Unfortunately, when the board decided to hold a national search and asked for the official credentials of the candidates, he submitted papers which were clearly counterfeit. When the chairman of the board investigated, he discovered that not only did the vice president lack the listed degrees, he lacked a bachelor's degree as well. In fact, he apparently had completed only one college course, English Composition. He received a grade of "C".

Imagine the ridicule. Imagine the embarrassment. If, reasoned the public, a man could do such a good job at a college with no degrees at all, what is the function of degrees? Where, they questioned, did all the money go that purportedly was from grants to the college? If he would lie about his education, would he not be inclined to steal money? Even though an audit by a highly respected firm showed no financial irregularity, the question was still there. In the meantime, the vice president had disappeared with his guns. People who loved him, and there were many, were fearful for his life. He returned, unharmed, and resigned. As his duplicity became real to the college staff, they went through the stages of grieving for him, themselves, and their college

The board of trustees offered me the position as Kirtland's fifth president in June of 1990, just three months after the academic scandal had been uncovered. And, while I knew the college's financial condition was desperate, I did not know how desperate. Added to both those issues is the fact that I am a middle-aged woman whose previous job was vice president for an institution in southern California. "California Woman Chosen as Kirtland's President," or just "Woman Selected as Kirtland's New President" were typical of the headlines of our local (weekly) papers. Only much later was I to learn how revolutionary the board had been in selecting me.

It seemed to me that one of my first jobs was to get to know the staff and to act as a sort of cheerleader to improve morale. I began a series of luncheons with randomly selected faculty, classified, and managerial employees so that I could learn names, faces, and personalities. I also believed it was essential to develop the administrative staff into a team. On my first day on the job, I contacted a consultant to work with us in team-building as we attempted to redefine the college's mission and to set new goals. After the latter was completed by the administrative staff, the same activities were done by the Board and the college staff. Our newly-defined mission and goals were a result of input from the entire college.

Just as I was beginning to believe that we had enough spirit and will to begin to organize for a two- to three-year public relations campaign designed to convince the voters to agree to raise their taxes to support their local college, two things happened:

1. The state, in a fiscal crisis of its own, withheld our quarterly allocation.

2. A supposed $50,000 carryover from the previous year turned out to be a huge shortfall; a cash flow analysis indicated we would not be able to make payroll in the early fall of the coming academic year, which was to be the beginning of my second year on the job.

After a series of emergency meetings with the staff and Board, we decided that we had to go out for a millage election as soon as possible. We also decided that we had to lay off several staff members in order to stay alive, financially, through the election. One of the administrative staff had the computer skills and program evaluation skills to precisely cost out each program and service and to describe each program's effect on the other. If nursing were canceled, for example, biology, chemistry, and English would lose most of their enrollments. This "ripple effect" is a concept seldom considered when attempting to decide which programs to cancel. We were able to prioritize all programs by cost, ripple effect, and by the degree to which they were essential to the college's mission. Since we are a learning institution, we wished to preserve the instructional area as long as possible.

In the end, 30% of our staff, mainly secretaries and custodians, were laid off in the summer of 1991, very near the anniversary of my first year as Kirtland's president. After that sad turn of events, the remainder of the college staff had to build up the enthusiasm to fight for the college's life. With little time to develop a strategy, we decided to flood the communities with speakers, each bearing a "fact sheet" answering questions we knew would be asked and telling our constituents what Kirtland does for each and every citizen. (Example: Even if you are a senior citizen who retired up here after raising and educating your children, Kirtland provides almost all the nurses and police and firefighters for the district. Kirtland's survival *does* affect you.)

It was also determined that an "off-the-wall" date might help the voters to remember the election date. We picked Friday the 13th of September 1991. We had telephone campaigns run by college, community and board people. We said we would go anywhere at anytime to spread Kirtland's message, and we did. I carried a six-pack of pop everywhere, which I would raise overhead after each speech to show how much the millage would cost the average property owner: $3.30 a month. In a final burst of commitment, two of the college's managers spoke at the dedication of a sanitary landfill the night before the election. I tell them they still glow orange.

Every time I write, talk, or read about the events that led up to the millage election, I get the same anxieties we all had to some degree: nausea, sleeplessness, racing heart, etc. After the polls closed on Friday the 13th, the whole staff waited for the results at my house. I honestly believed what had been advertised as either a wild celebration or a "wake" would in fact be the latter.

As the evening progressed, and the news called in by townships showed we had a landslide, the joy we felt is indescribable. The celebration marked the beginning of the new era of financial stability and a whole new world of opportunity for Kirtland Community College and the people of our district.

Would I do it again? Yes.

Dorothy Franke is President of Kirtland Community College in Roscommon, MI. She has presented at the League for Innovation conference and is also a member of the "New Directions for Michigan's Community Colleges" commission.

8

The Media

Another group to whom public college presidents have become accountable, by demand and not by choice, is the press. The need of the college to publicize events, programs, and special services always is balanced against the need of the news media to sell papers, which many believe they can do only by reporting controversy no matter how minor or insignificant. So, we need the press in one way, and they need us in another. Sometimes it can be a love-hate relationship, but whether presidents like it or not, there *will* be a relationship of some kind.

There seems to be a trend that continues to develop in this society as a result of the increased demand for "news," the rapidity with which information can be transmitted throughout the world, and a basic voyeuristic/iconoclastic element that seems to be a part of human nature.

DEMAND FOR QUANTITY

The demand for something to write about and especially something to talk about on television and radio has resulted in the escalation of many unmemorable and local events into the "crises of the week." While celebrities have long been the subjects of articles in the print media and on television, lately the celebrity net has widened to include every person ever involved in a crime or a heroic rescue or a steamy love affair. From supermarkets flaunting publications such as *The National Enquirer* and all of its clones, to radio shows inviting callers to discuss everything imaginable, to one hundred and one television shows based on the experiences of "real people," we have almost buried our society in verbiage and amateur videotape footage. One of the most frightening things I have read is that with all of the advancements in fiber optic technology, we will soon have the capability of simultaneously airing 500 television channels. While I am on the one hand enchanted by the wonders of the human minds which create such technology, I am at the same time appalled at its general application and the at implications for our future. Is there no limit to what we need to know about everyone else's business? Is there no limit to what we need to know about our public figures or elected officials? Is there no limit to how many times we can take a true story and turn it into a documentary and then into a movie and then into a television series of the same name and then publish it as a paperback book just in case anyone missed one of the earlier versions? How many times can "The Brady Bunch" or "I Love Lucy" or "M*A*S*H" be rerun on any one of 500 channels? How many specialized publications or television channels can we really absorb?

It is as though the more we know, the less we understand. The more specialized our sources of information become, the less we are able to communicate with those whose interests and backgrounds are different from ours. The more computer literate we become, the less we talk to each other face to face. And the more we are subjected to the same stories day after day and week after week, the less we listen and the shorter our attention span becomes. I fear that the glut of "information" is making us deaf and blind to the wisdom of the ages which is all that will allow us to survive as a civilization.

SPEED OF TRANSMISSION

The rapidity with which information is transmitted around the globe is also a part of the exponential demand for something to transmit. It has also added a sense of urgency and intensity that is addictive. The Gulf War is a good example of this phenomenon. There may have only been thousands of troops in the Gulf, but there were millions of people watching the war as it happened. We saw the missiles fired into the night sky; we saw the bombs dropped from the vantage point of the pilots and navigators; we were perched on the tanks as they lumbered over sand dunes; we were surrounded by the smoke from the oil wells set on fire and touched by the oil spilling into the water. Millions of Americans are veterans of that war because we could watch it on television as it was happening. What we were not able to personally witness was then told to us by highly controlled military press conferences which were the diametric opposite of the television personalities reporting the evening news while all hell broke loose behind them. Yet even the press conferences were held immediately after the completion of some major offensive or significant raid. We had more information about this war than perhaps any other in history. But how much do we *understand* about the war or why it even happened? It feels as though the details of the activity have buried the meaning and significance of it. I wonder if that war would have been waged if we had less of a need for political image making and posturing in a world bound together by satellite-transmitted images and fiber optic networks.

Our National Addiction to News

The third characteristic which is driving the media trend as much as the demand for information and the capability to deliver that information as it happens, is an insatiable appetite we humans have for common garden-variety, back-fence gossip. Small towns have always been noted for everyone knowing everyone else's business. Now that the world is technologically just another small town, we get to gossip on a grand and global scale. Any public action of any individual is a target for someone writing or talking for an audience. In addition, the private activities of those thought to be public persona are even more desirable targets for the writers and talkers. There are so many examples to choose from under this heading that it is unnecessary to elaborate—we all have many examples from our own lives that we can fill in. In general, however, it seems as though this particular aspect of human nature has become more vicious because everything is justified by the media as "the public's right to know." I feel that in my generation, the roots of the present "expose" trend can be traced back to Deep Throat, Bob Woodward, and Carl Bernstein. Prior to Watergate, public officials were treated a bit more respectfully by the media. In the years since Watergate, many innocent—as well as many guilty—public figures have been skewered by investigative reporters.

The oral tradition of the ancient cultures produced many stories which were told not only for their entertainment value but also for their truths that became evident within the framework of the stories. We are missing that last ingredient in much of what consumes us as it is transmitted by today's news media. They believe they are dealing with truth when often in fact they are only distracting from the truth by dramatizing what is not dramatic, by creating conflict where none exists, or by focusing on events which only perpetuate myths and do not examine beneath the surface. I still have an article from a newspaper in a small town in Wyoming whose headlines blazed on the front page about a shooting incident that day on the local reservation. Yet the article stated that the person who was supposedly doing the shooting could not be identified; witnesses to the shooting could not be found; and the place where the shooting took place was unknown. The only basis for the headline and article which took up much of the front page was a reporter who was ready to believe that, as usual, the savage Shoshones and Arapahos were out there trying to kill each other. The myth was given new life under the guise of being "news" which the law-abiding citizens of the area had a "right to know."

MEDIA-PRESIDENT RELATIONS

In this kind of environment it is no wonder that many community college presidents can feel besieged by the press. We don't always know how to behave when we are asked to respond to events or situations involving the college. In spite of the fact that our public relations offices produce hundreds of press releases per year to publicize what we are doing in and for the community, there will be those occasions when the press may decide that something we are doing is more newsworthy than we believe it to be. And there will be occasions when someone who is disgruntled with our college will either write letters to the editor which get published or will find a reporter eager to uncover a scandal.

One logical expectation is that interactions between presidents and the press may be difficult for the reasons just mentioned: the media has to have something to write and talk about, and the preference is that it be something controversial; and they want to be able to report events as they happen, especially if they might be sordid or potentially dramatic. Public officials and public institutions are being held to a more rigid standard now that we are competing more vigorously for shrinking resources. As long as the public remains in its "no new taxes" mode, especially until waste and fraud are eliminated from government, then everything our colleges do and everything we do as presidents is going to be put under the journalistic microscope.

An article that appeared in *Newsweek* right after the election of President Clinton makes a point about the government which can also be applied to our circumstances in smaller entities such as community colleges. Robert Samuelson, in an essay appearing on February 1, 1993, wrote about how the major problem the new president will have to confront is the "modern welfare state." He defines the modern welfare state as the government which provides almost all of us with various types of benefits, takes huge chunks of our personal income, and creates a "vast web of dependency...that is the ultimate source of huge budget deficits and, quite perversely, distrust of government." Because the government has taken on the responsibility for so many, he says, it has ultimately also incurred the wrath of the many because dependency creates a backlash. "Paradoxically, government's very generosity helps make it unpopular. Government does so much for so many that anyone can find something that seems wrong or unneeded. My benefit is public-spirited necessity; yours is ill-conceived waste." (p.51) This is an interesting analysis of the problems we face in the future in this country. It also parallels our situations as presidents of public institutions facing our most serious fiscal mandate ever.

One could call community colleges the higher education institutions of the modern welfare state, using Samuelson's definition. Founded as "democracy's colleges," our mandate has been to try to meet every need of every person in our service area. We are the primary providers of developmental education for those who didn't learn enough the first time around. We are the providers of the first level of the baccalaureate education. We are the providers of technical education. We are the providers of job training and upgrading for displaced workers as well as for those in business and industry. We are the providers of recreational learning opportunities for those with leisure time they wish to fill more productively. In many communities we are the providers of the physical space—theaters, field houses, concert halls, athletic fields, classrooms—for other groups to utilize because they have no where else to gather. Therefore, we are the providers in those same communities of entertainment and culture as well as of classroom education. We provide child care for our students and staffs. We provide cafeterias and bookstores which are open to the general public. And we provide a place of employment for hundreds or thousands of people in our respective areas.

It should not be surprising, then, that as we have found ourselves with less money but with constant or increased demands to respond to every need, we are perfect targets for the public outpouring of anger or resentment if anything we must curtail impinges on the special interests of anyone we have pledged to serve in the past. Thus, the ingredients for confrontation, which will be eagerly courted by the news media, are laying in the lap of the president. In imitation of Mr. Samuelson, our students and employees are saying, "My program or job is public-spirited necessity; yours is ill-conceived waste." Furthermore, "If you (the institution, a.k.a. President So-and So) don't do what I want, then I will go to the press and bring public pressure to bear until you change your mind."

There are various theories about how to behave when something potentially negative happens on our campuses. I honestly don't know what the answers are, but I do know that most presidents are becoming more and more leery of being open and honest with the media. None of us will advocate trying to hide something or cover up something (remember Nixon?), but all of us have to find our own comfort level in providing information just because it is requested. Some believe that it is best to be cooperative; others will say that most times the best answer to a reporter who is searching for something is a simple "I have no comment." It is the equivalent of turning the other cheek; if we refuse to participate in the making of a "fight," then whatever the reporter wants to say or write is diminished. There is much wisdom in Mark Twain's comment about it being better to keep one's mouth shut and be thought a fool than to open it and remove all doubt. It may be part of the president's role to defend the institution, but it is not good for the institution *or* the individual for the president to be defensive. It is part of our job to brag about our college, but the college is not helped if we talk so much that we are seen as braggarts.

Again, the key is maintaining a balance. None of us likes to be criticized publicly, especially by those whom we believe have no understanding of what we do or of the constraints under which we have to make decisions. Second guessing has almost replaced baseball as the national pastime. But our dislike of it is not going to stop the commentary, so we need at least to expect it from time to time and learn to deal with it.

What will Interest the Media

The general issues which will continue to be lightning rods for the media will include budgetary decisions involving reductions in personnel; other personnel issues—particularly terminations; salary increases—especially for presidents and other administrators; improprieties which may be uncovered as a result of a routine audit; acts of violence on the campus; substance abuse on the campus; and any topic involving athletics. These are the things that newspapers in particular assume that people in our communities care about: jobs, money, crime, and sports. In addition, most presidents will agree that the stories as reported invariably will be slanted in favor of an aggrieved individual and against an institution. There is something about the American mentality that loves an underdog and relishes in personal triumphs against "the system."

In spite of these problematic areas, a president can never allow the institution to be managed by the press. We have to be conscious of the consequences of our decisions and how they might get reported, but under no circumstances can we allow any distaste we might have for public scrutiny to deter us from doing what we know is best for the college as a whole. If we have acted in good faith, if we have been honest, and if we have made the best decision we could given the information we had available to us, then we have to simply wait out whatever negative media commentary may follow. And as presidents, we must also guide our local boards so that they do not succumb to the temptation of making poor decisions just to avoid conflict in the community or potentially negative publicity.

Roger Andersen, president of Adirondack Community College, recently wrote in *The Community College Times* some good advice for institutional response to a campus crisis (December 1, 1992). His important points to remember include saying you don't know when that is the truth; never lying; treating all reporters equally; not over-reacting or becoming defensive; and maintaining a record of everyone spoken to from the media for future reference. Andersen advises, "Credibility and sincerity are a college leader's strongest assets. Protect them by always telling the truth. Those speaking for the college should not try to manage the news. Withholding, avoiding, or 'massaging' the truth does far more harm than good." (p. 2)

As stated earlier, there will always be a relationship between the president and the news media because we need each other, even if for different reasons. The press can be our greatest supporters, and they can be our worst nightmare. Regardless, the media is an important fact of our lives as we deal with increasingly complex choices. In addition, the continuing tendency to simplify everything into sound bites, no matter what the topic, is having an impact on how we deliver education to our students, most of whom are veterans themselves of this television-dominated society. Therefore, as those who provide leadership in our institutions, we must constantly be aware of the media presence in all of our lives, celebrating what we have been brought as a result and fighting against what, if left unattended, has the potential to destroy all we have worked so hard to create.

Part III

Developing the Job

Ultimately one cannot write about being a president without examining some of the day-to-day activities in which a president is engaged. This then leads to a examination of issues raised in the first part of this discussion: What is it that separates an effective president from an ineffective one? What type of person is more likely to function well in the position? And finally, is there going to be a difference in the type of person who will be an effective president in 2000 from the one who was effective in 1980 or in the 1990s?

9

Describing the Job and Setting Priorities

THE JOB

I am always at a loss when someone making small talk asks me what I do. Beyond stating the obvious, the title of my job, often I haven't known what else to say. What is it that a president *does*?

On any given day in the life of a community college president, that person will: have individual appointments with at least four people; chair or attend at least one meeting with more than one person; answer or initiate approximately ten phone calls; write or dictate three letters; read through ten or fifteen individual pieces of mail, many of which require a response of some kind; toss out twenty other pieces of mail that don't require a response but which must be read in order to figure that out; sign onto a computer system to receive and send electronic mail messages; attend one meeting off-campus as a representative of the college to some community group; start stacking things to take home that don't have to be read immediately but must be read later—such as journals and periodicals; snatch a few minutes to search for materials to put together for that speech in the next day or two.

On those days when the president is off-campus for the day (as presidents are, for example, one and often two days per week), the phone messages, electronic mail messages, and stacks of mail seem to triple for every day away. So, more "stuff" gets dragged home to be sorted, evaluated, and absorbed or thrown out. If none of this sounds glamorous, that is because it isn't. There is routine to any position in an organization, including that of the presidency.

Although the job of president has a certain amount of routine activity, there is also much that is unpredictable in any day. The unpredictable always happens. Even when blocks of time are set aside in the schedule, they will often evaporate like the morning mist. It is difficult, if not impossible, to work on sustained projects in the office.

It is the non-routine aspect of the job that most of us find the most rewarding, the most stimulating, and sometimes the most difficult. You just never know when a fire truck or ambulance is going to scream into view, or when a boiler is going to break, or when any one of a cast of thousands might drop by to alert you to a potential problem, or just to say hello, or to ask for an immediate decision or a signature on a grant application which has to be sent out *that day*. Or, there might be that dreaded fax from the politicians or the central office telling you that—with regret—you are being asked to cut another 3% from your operating budget, effective immediately.

Most presidents will agree that a typical day involves too many activities and too many tasks to be accomplished in too short a time frame. It might be more productive to look, therefore, at characteristics of personality which may be more important than the way one manages one's time. In order to be able to cope with the demands just mentioned, it helps to be mentally active, energetic, and able to work in the midst of chaos.

PERSONALITY THEORY

In the 1970s, two Canadian researchers named Hunt and Sullivan wrote about the conceptual levels on which people function. Their theories are built upon those of many others, including Piaget, Buner, Gagne, Rogers and Maslow. The basic concept is that in addition to other types of growth, humans develop at various rates and to various levels of cognitive functioning. They created a short test to determine one's level of complexity in thinking. That test consists of having subjects answer six open-ended questions about how they respond to being told what to do, or how they feel about their parents, for example. Test scores reveal that people function in ranges from the very simple, where the world is seen in terms of black/white, right/wrong, yes/no, to the very complex, where decisions and judgments are based on circumstances revealed, where evidence of synthesizing and evaluating are apparent in the thinking process. Those in the midrange of what Hunt and Sullivan call cognitive complexity function at very concrete levels in some situations and more abstract levels in others. There are obvious parallels which can be drawn to Bloom's taxonomy and to Kohlberg's theories of moral development, but what is interesting professionally is to apply the cognitive complexity theory to community college faculty and staff, including presidents.

For example, we probably want our financial aid officers and business office personnel to be more concrete than abstract thinkers. Creativity in these areas can have serious consequences. We *want* them to see the world in terms of black and white or right and wrong, to "follow the rules" until told not to by a higher authority or until the rules change and are published in the *Federal Register*.

On the other hand, it may also be that we want others in the organization to function at greater levels of complexity because their worlds are more abstract: the student development team, the counselor working with the disabled or disadvantaged, the career counselor, the academic advisor. These are all positions which require an ability to put information together in new ways "on the spot" to serve the needs of a given individual. Obviously there are still rules and regulations which must be followed, but since each situation will be different due to the individuality of each student or situation, people who are counselors and student advisors must be able to accept the fact that there *is* no right or wrong answer, no black or white choice in many situations. They must be able to tolerate a certain level of ambiguity in what they do and in what they counsel or advise.

And what about the community college president? It could be argued that the most effective presidents are those who also have a very high tolerance for ambiguity and who understand shades of gray. They must operate most times at a fairly high level of cognitive complexity because no two situations are alike and no two circumstances will exactly resemble each other. This does not mean, however, that we are not also responsible for maintaining some level of consistency within the organization. There have to be dependable codes of behavior which are the same for everyone, regardless of position or rank. There also have to be consistencies imposed so that all doesn't become chaos every day. The president is the one, however, who is responsible for knowing when to insist on order and when to allow exceptions. That requires a very high level of tolerance for ambiguity as well as a high level of tolerance for the frustration felt when circumstances dictate going against what is right or reasonable.

To illustrate my point I can use a minor event that occurred when I had been a president only for about four months. The week before Thanksgiving I was asked a question in a staff meeting about whether or not it would be possible to let offices close by 2:30 or 3:00 so that people could go home and have a less hurried start to the holiday. It seemed like a reasonable request to me because I had also discovered that the Friday after Thanksgiving, a day that I had always had as a holiday too, was in fact not a holiday at my college. I stated that it would be fine with me if people wanted to leave early. What I thought was an innocuous request and something easy to do for people became something far different and caused an enormous and immediate response from some members of the classified staff. The question was raised by the union steward about what I intended to do for those who didn't come to work until 2:00, or for the security guards who worked the midnight shift. Would they also be entitled to two or three hours off? And if not, should anybody have the time off, especially administrators? I learned very quickly the need for consistency in decision-making among those who for the most part are not expected to think on a highly complex level. The result was that we did not close early, everyone worked a full day, and my attempt to be generous was a dismal failure. (That was when I first heard the statement, "No good deed goes unpunished.") More importantly, I have become much more cognizant of the differences in employees' needs and expectations. The president is the one who sets the tone for fairness, for consistency, and for predictability. And yet the president is also the one who must be able to live in an environment where often there are no answers which are clear cut and few which are obvious.

I also worked for almost two years in an art school as the equivalent to the academic dean. As interesting as it was there because of the multitude of truly creative and inventive people, there was also a tension that will never be resolved because the needs of the institution dictated the maintenance of structure to process paper, to meet accrediting standards, to obey the law by adhering to course and class schedules, or to have faculty do things such as write syllabi. As a group, these artists were not very amenable to structure, or to rules and deadlines not created by their own impulses. Their identity was "artist", not "faculty member". Thus, it always felt as though there was a certain lack of continuity or commitment to sustained activity seen as necessary from the management side but as a complete anathema to those who supplemented their income as artists by teaching classes. Their students also were usually just like them and just as difficult to keep on track in the traditional academic sense. Imagine the fun in the registrar's office or in financial aid. My job was to prod, to mediate, and to try to keep everything intact academically. I often felt I was a Sheltie herding everyone rather than a Bloodhound leading anyone anywhere. If the complexity theory is correct, the choice at that institution is to continue to hire non-artists like myself to be the managers, knowing that the only other option is to promote from within and try to make managers out of artists. The inherent tension will always exist because of the very nature of the place and the people who fill its halls.

Even though no one has scientifically tested this theory about cognitive complexity among community college employees, it does seem plausible. Furthermore, it is also plausible that organizations become dysfunctional when an employee operating at a more concrete level is placed in a position requiring more abstract thinking, or when someone who is highly creative and abstract is put in a position which requires structure and routine all the time.

ORGANIZATIONAL THEORY

Most of our community colleges have similar issues which, if not understandable viewed through complexity or personality theories, might be understood as Mintzberg tried to explain them (1979) in his analysis of the professional bureaucracy, of which community colleges are a part. He attributes the tension in organizations to the impulses of the different parts pulling against each other for power and for influence. For example, the faculty ("the operating core") wants to control the institution by controlling curricular decision-making, which then drives everything else. The student services people deal with individual students and want exceptions made to the rules all the time in order to accommodate individual needs. That drives the business office folks crazy because they are intensely trying to make everyone follow the same rules and behave in a predictable manner. Meanwhile, the president and the deans and the board are struggling to hang onto their power and influence by insisting that more and more decisions get made at the top, as though that will solve problems and provide consistency. After all, aren't they the only ones who actually know what is going on throughout the institution and know what all the various pressures are?

However organizational behavior is explained, it again gets back to individual differences and the types of people who drift to certain professions. Since one of the tasks of the president is to maintain a balance in the organization to ensure that it neither crashes into chaos nor petrifies with structure, it is an enormous help if the president has the capacity to be adaptable—to handle the routine tasks of the job without being buried and to adjust to the unexpected or the creative challenge of the moment without being panicked because the event was not predicted. It also helps not to take it all too seriously. There just isn't enough time.

SETTING PRIORITIES

Of course there are many constituencies which compete for the attention of the president: faculty, students, the general public; other specific staff groups such as clerical staff, part- time staff, grant-funded staff; boards and central offices in whatever form they exist from state to state; legislators both at the state and local levels; and friends and family of the president. In addition to people, there are also things to be considered, some of which have already been mentioned: routine tasks such as dealing with the mountains of paper that mysteriously appear on the desk every day; correspondence; responses to requests from others; responsibilities related to community and professional roles played outside the institution but on behalf of the institution; and of course, responses to the crisis of the moment. Every president I have ever talked with has agreed that there is simply too much to be done by a president and that one of the hardest parts of the job is knowing how to assign priority to those tasks. This is particularly difficult for the new president, but remains an issue regardless of how long we're in the job. I concur with those observations and while my particular style would not fit everyone, there are some general conclusions I have drawn about how to determine how I spend my time.

Something that impressed me about another president I once worked for was that anything that had to be signed by him was never in his office more than twenty-four hours (as long as he was physically on campus). I have tried to maintain the same standard, knowing how important it is to others' schedules that requisitions or final actions not be delayed by my neglect. I always assume that since I am the last one to see requests in their written form and that proposals have been reviewed by many others before they get to me, the time line on which we are operating when I get involved is relatively short. Therefore, as a courtesy to staff I make it a priority to move things through my office as quickly as possible so that they can do their jobs of making things happen. Obviously there are exceptions. I will not act on something until I am sure of what is being proposed, and the process I must go through to feel comfortable with a decision can take some time. But when dealing with the more routine tasks of the organization, there is no excuse for the president's office to be the source of delay.

In that there are so many campus groups wanting the attention of the president, it seems obvious that a major portion of a president's time must be devoted to dealing with campus issues and attending meetings, or providing time for individual appointments. The dilemma is that choices still have to be made, the result of which is that the person or group who has to wait for several days for a meeting/appointment can feel slighted or less important. The simple truth is that not every issue has the same weight to the organization, and the president is the one who either directly or indirectly must decide on what topics will be given the most or the timeliest attention. Again, this is the hardest type of distinction for a new president to learn but one of the most important. For me the answer lies again in the concept of balance. The president must be careful not to become too absorbed in any one topic of discussion because if that happens, then there are too many other issues which get ignored or dealt with by default. In one sense, I have discovered that as a president I have had to abandon any inclination I might have had to be compulsive. When I first started this job, I compared it to driving on a freeway during rush-hour traffic while trying to eat a seven course meal. While it still feels that way most of the time, I have become more acclimated to the pace. All of those years of schooling, in which the value of "finishing what you begin" was ingrained, have led to a job in which nothing is ever finished, nothing is ever tied up in a neat package, and little ever reaches closure.

Among the issues Kerr and Gade (1986) discovered in interviewing new presidents, there were several common experiences, including the sense of being driven by phone calls not returned, letters not answered, persons not seen—even in a 60 to 80 hour week. They also found that presidents were dissatisfied with the lack of time to read and think. It is no wonder that when presidents have a chance to work on a building project, for example, they jump at it. At least there will be results that can be seen and touched and smelled. But while that building is getting built, or while the funds are being raised to build it, if we are not careful other equally important issues which need attention may flounder or get resolved in ways which negate everything good that the building represents.

While all presidents have preferences for how to spend their time, we must be very careful not to let ourselves be dominated by any one project, or by the agenda of any one person or any one group. Another way of looking at this issue is to think about the criticism of Jimmy Carter as President. He was educated as an engineer, which indicates that he was both trained and inclined to see projects through from beginning to end and to concentrate on every detail along the way. That is how we want engineers to behave. But that mode of behavior and thinking, as it turned out, did not serve him well as president. Because he was so involved in the details of a few projects, he didn't have time to pay attention to important policy issues or to provide his staff with the leadership they wanted. As a result, others stepped into the vacuum and Carter basically lost control of and influence in his own administration. There is a lesson to be learned there for all presidents.

Adding to the pressure on a president to pay attention to many things at the same time are the demands made by those outside the institution. All of us, by virtue of the position, get involved in quite a few community projects and get invited to many other events. In a small community the pressure is even greater to be at every event and be a member of every board of directors imaginable. The demands are constant and unrelenting. But again, choices have to be made, and the president must weigh what is important to the college, what is of interest to the individual, and what might have to wait until a later date.

There is no solution, short of cloning, to the daily dilemma we face about where to put our energies. Furthermore, since every college is as different as every president (and as similar), the choices cannot be made in advance. There is no graduate course that tells a president how to set priorities. A lot of it has to do with the situation, the nature of the community, and the needs of the college. What is important for us to remember is that we all face the same choices and issues. I find it comforting that even when I am as stretched to my limit, I know there are at least 1000 other community college presidents out there who have felt the same things and experienced the same pressures. It helps keep it all in perspective, even if it doesn't add any hours to the length of the day.

One last comment about setting priorities is that I have finally learned that there aren't many things which won't wait over night. Yes, there are crises. Yes, there are deadlines. Yes, there are all those meetings to attend. But in our zeal to do our jobs, we cannot let ourselves lose track of time in an abstract sense. I make better decisions when I have had some time to think about things. Even knowing that, it is extremely difficult not to give in to others' sense of urgency or to their agendas and timetables. The world has not yet come to an end because I didn't get everything I intended to do done in one day. The college has not closed because the president has been unavailable for a few hours or a few days. So, as we set priorities, it is good to remember that we are but one of the players in the game, not the game itself.

Clearly there are many more questions to be asked—and answered—about the community college president's profession. While on the one hand there is nothing mysterious about the job, on the other there is no way one can truly prepare for it. It is also hard to accurately write about it. However, there are some common threads in all of the literature as well as in our personal experiences which have led to some conclusions and speculations about community college presidents and community college presidencies.

One often-expressed opinion is that the job is an impossible one because nothing is ever finished. In addition, the increasing complexity of the position has made it more and more difficult to find the time necessary for the reflection which leads to better decision-making. It has also become more difficult for presidents to ever really get away. Most vacations are interrupted by periodic phone calls to the campus. In this age of instant access, car telephones and beepers are common intruders on thought, and modems and lap tops have made it possible to utilize every waking moment for college business. Thus, perhaps one of the characteristics that a successful president must possess could be described as enough self-discipline to know when to be unavailable and enough strength of will to turn the computer *off*. Every president I have ever known—myself included— regrets that there is not more time to pursue personal interests.

Even when we identify blocks of time to spend on one activity, it is often consumed by furiously reading professional and related publications or books just to try to keep up with what is going on. For example, if we are to understand anything about the world we are supposedly preparing our students to inhabit, then we must understand the impact of technology on everyday life, we must understand the economic consequences of events around the globe, and we must understand the increasing social pressures brought to bear on all of us. "I must hurry and catch up with the others, for I am their leader" is a statement that has serious meaning beneath its facetious surface.

Essay

A BALANCED LIFE
by Byron McClenney

The people attracted to the community college presidency tend to be motivated by achievement. They also tend to be somewhat competitive. When those characteristics are brought to an institution constantly striving for appropriate recognition in the world of higher education, it is likely to produce the classic workaholic. The necessary community involvements coupled with the internal needs of any institution produce a climate which encourages or even demands that one work long days and weekends to master the situation. All of the above can be further complicated if politics play an important role in the day to day affairs of the institution.

As one who has completed 22 years as a community college president or chancellor, I can reflect on several defining events which caused me to develop some balance in my life. They were the type of startling events which cause a fundamental re-examination of what is really important at the personal and professional levels. These events are the ones leading to exasperation because maximum effort and long hours are not enough. Total commitment and significant achievements are not enough.

I will never forget the experience of being summoned to the office of the board chairman on a Saturday morning. I had just taken a seat when we were joined by another board member. They proceeded to discuss a list of administrators they did not want me to recommend for new contracts. Their message was that they would never again bother me in the personnel arena if I would just take care of these matters. The problem was that the list included my most competent administrators who could be trusted to be ethical under any circumstances. They were the ones who were working the long hours and weekends at my side to try to make a difference under the most difficult circumstances. Needless to say, the situation led to a fundamental re-examination of what is important. The administrators did receive new contracts, but not without a price being paid by the CEO.

Another of those defining events happened as I was considering the non-renewal of a contract for a top administrator who had long before stopped being productive. He owned a private business where he spent too much time and frequently went to sleep in meetings. A different board chair endeavored to save his job by challenging my recommendation. I will never forget her assertion that if the administrator had not been caught stealing, then we probably did not have cause to take the recommended action. Here was another of those times when I needed to decide what was important and think about the price to be paid. The administrator did not receive a new contract.

While there have been other professional experiences similar to those described, the last defining event I will describe was at a more personal level. A diagnosis of cancer which led to radical surgery also led to a fundamental re-examination of what is important in life. Where the other experiences caused me to introduce some balancing elements, this experience pushed me to a deeper level of thinking about how to view all of life. I can recall reviewing in my mind all of the forces and factors that motivate or compel us to do the things we do as community college executives.

I thought about all of my family relationships and the way I spend my time. I recalled all the dreams I had not yet experienced in real life. What emerged was an even stronger sense of the importance of balance in all aspects of life. I completed the transition begun several years before from 12-hour days to 9-hour days on the average. That is not to say that one can or should avoid evening events or weekend activities. It is to say that if there is not a breakfast event on the calendar then it is possible to arrive in the office a little later than usual. It is also to say that after a particularly stressful day it may be appropriate to take off early and go home to work in the garden or whatever one does to relax.

I was asked not long ago to produce a quote which could be used in a publication. What I wrote was the following:

> Life is too short to spend it dwelling on negative thoughts or with negative people. Living, learning, loving, and laughing will occupy my days if I have my way. Reading, gardening, and travel provide some of my most pleasant moments and memories.

What I realize as I reread the statement is the extent to which I have transformed the way I approach work. If anything, I feel more productive than ever before, but I no longer feel as though I need to carry the burdens of the world on my shoulders.

The attitudes people bring to their work and the way they organize their work can have a major impact on whether or not people have lives outside their professional roles. A review of my years as a college president reveals a list of important items I have always been concerned about as I organize work for my organization. The "Top Ten" are:

1. Lead the institution to create a collective vision for itself

2. Develop strategies for future development

3. Create priorities for the near term

4. Allocate resources to implement plans

5. Create a collaborative spirit within the institution

6. Hire good people and get out of the way

7. Solve small problems to avoid crises

8. Keep the institution student-centered

9. Always respond promptly and honestly to the press

10. Keep a "To Do" list and start each day with the important task that is the most difficult

While it is obvious a person can do all of the above and still work 12-hour days, the sense of priorities which can emerge will provide the opportunity to work 9-hour days. If one feels confident that he or she is aware of what is the next most important task, then it is possible to be focused and even intense if necessary. Anyone who has ever been a chief executive knows the work is never finished, but real control and comfort come when the suggested approaches drive the way one approaches work.

Some administrators create crises by the way they work, and some seem to thrive when they are dealing with one crisis after another because then they know they are needed. All of these people will have great difficulty working less than 12-hour days. What I know from experience in four very different settings is that it is possible to help administrators, faculty, and staff to feel they can control their own destinies. As people begin to feel the resulting power, the chief executive can function more like the conductor of an orchestra. As fine tuning occurs over time, the number of crises will diminish.

I refuse to have a telephone in my car, carry a pager, or call the office every day when I am on vacation. All of those things communicate important messages to people within an institution. They also free a president to enjoy life outside the office or the professional circle of activities. There will also be fewer divorces, happier children, and healthier presidents if the people who fill those roles can develop balance between the professional role and the private life.

Most of the significant others like spouses, partners, children, and friends would like to see college presidents and chancellors achieve some balance. Enlightened board members should want the same for the chief executive. Just as seat time for students is not the most important criterion, hours on the job is not the most important measure of success for presidents. At a time when change is the only constant, working smarter rather than harder will provide the key to success.

If all I am is what I do as a professional then what is left when I am no longer a chief executive? If relationships are not nurtured and my health is broken, how can I enjoy the next stages of life? While I have enjoyed 22 years of satisfaction as a leader for four different community colleges, the quest for balance in life will be on my agenda for the next 12-15 years which I hope to serve as a chief executive.

Byron McClenney is President of the Community College of Denver in Colorado. He has also served as the Chancellor of the Alamo Community College District in San Antonio, TX and has been a member of the American Association of Community Colleges Board of Directors. He has served on numerous other commissions and professional boards.

10

Where We Have Been, Where We Are Going

Many have observed that the first generation of community college presidents included the builders of buildings, the courtiers of politicians to get funding, the architects of the organizational structure borrowed from our sibling universities and colleges. Indeed, that first generation of presidents who opened the doors of one campus per week in the late 60s and early 70s started to create something new— the open door institution—but they borrowed old concepts and ideas with which they were familiar: the core must be liberal arts and transfer programs. One example close to my heart is that the college of which I was first a president was founded by a man who graduated from Dartmouth. People there believe that he proudly set about creating a "little Dartmouth" and that he pretty much succeeded. It is now thirty-three years later but the spirit of that first president is alive and well (as is he, teaching on the west coast) and many of the faculty he hired in his seventeen plus years at the helm are still there, still believing that they are becoming a "little Dartmouth." I also remember when I was a community college teacher that I felt some of my colleagues still hadn't recovered from the discovery that they were at a small community college and not at Harvard. It seriously affected how they treated students and how they treated each other. But we must remember the likely source of their beliefs: it came not only from their *experiences* but also from their *leaders.*

The first chapter of a book written about community colleges is entitled "What in the World is a Community College?" and begins, "In September of 1960 I found myself running an educational bedlam. It was called a community college." (O'Connell, 1968). It is really no mystery why those founding presidents and faculty drew upon what was familiar to them to convert this bedlam to something out of which they could make some sense. Even while drawing on the accepted baccalaureate model, there was still a recognition that something was changing. O'Connell also wrote the following:

> The community college is changing the definition of the word 'college.' It is also making obsolete the concept of considering young people to be of 'college material' or 'not college material.' The word 'college' is now something much broader, much more inclusive. (p. 34)

Finally, he spoke for many presidents in 1968 with the following conclusion to his book:

> A final word: in one important respect the community college president must be unique: he must have or develop a real commitment to the value of the two-year career or occupational programs. For he has a chance to lead his faculty and his somewhat inchoate institution into an area of service to society which will take on an increasing importance as time goes on and as more and more high school graduates move on to post-secondary education. So far, the community colleges have talked much better than they have performed in career or occupational education. We have not really yet begun to educate sub-professionals and technicians in anything like the numbers needed. We'd better start soon, and I think we will. The trick will be for our community colleges to remain flexible enough and zestful enough and imaginative enough to meet the special new educational needs of the United States which community colleges appear uniquely well-suited to handle. We must be, in fact as well as in name, 'a new college for a new society.' (p. 133-34)

This was the dream upon which community colleges were built by those first presidents, a dream which has been kept alive by all of us since that time.

The second generation of presidents, entering mostly in the late seventies, has been the one which has taken the original concept of community college and helped it to expand to include this other track for students: the non-transfer, more occupationally-oriented course of study. In addition to expanding programs to include more applied subjects and programs, this second generation of presidents often expanded campus physical plants. Community colleges moved out of inherited public school buildings into their own facilities, or added entire campuses to try to accommodate burgeoning enrollments.

These presidents also lived through other phenomena such as the implementation of faculty association bargaining unit contracts which explicitly spell out working conditions; the increasing politicizing of higher education as states form, reform, and reorganize their state systems; and the boom or bust funding cycles which have resulted in uneven progress in all areas of higher education—from program quality and availability to employee compensation. Many of these second generation presidents are still in the job even if not at the institution where they originally became college presidents. According to a study published in 1986, these presidents are symbols "of that group of Americans born of blue-collar homes, who either lived through the tail-end of the Great Depression or who had heard enough stories about it to influence forever their values." (Vaughan, 1986) Vaughan also states that these presidents are, therefore, "philosophically, emotionally, and, in some cases, spiritually geared to serve as presidents of 'the people's college'." What is not stated is that these presidents are also predominately white and male, as were those in the first generation.

Generally speaking, I consider myself part of the third generation of presidents. More of us are female (11%), more of us are minority, and more of us grew up after the Depression, and after World War II (the median age in 1992 was 52). Even though I have been a part of the community college movement since 1970 and vaguely remember the years of dramatic growth in the sheer numbers of community colleges, I have been a president only since the mid-eighties, so perhaps the recent changes seem more dramatic than they really are. A colleague (a second generation) who has been in this profession for many years states that there is nothing new and " everything we have experienced in the past five years has happened before and will happen again". On the one hand, what he is saying is true. Not much about human nature changes from day to day, or century to century for that matter. On the other hand, also true is that this entire country is entering a new phase and as a result, community colleges are going to be different institutions in the future from what we are right now. We are in a time which is changing not only who our students are, but also how we are financed and organized. In addition, the impact of technology cannot be underestimated. It is one of the primary forces shaping how we interact, how we organize, and how we educate.

THE IDEAL FOR THE FUTURE

There still may be nothing more difficult for a community college president than adequately preparing the institution for a future which grows more and more uncertain as the days pass. At the 1993 Summer Experience for Community College Presidents which is sponsored by the Presidents Academy of the American Association of Community Colleges, fifty presidents gathered together to discuss the future: what it may become, how we can respond as citizens, and how we *must* respond as community college leaders.

THE FUTURE OF SOCIETY

The discussion started with Robert Theobald, a futurist who has written extensively about the forces which have shaped the past and the changing forces which must shape the future if we are to survive. He has stated that we will move in one of two directions, either toward a more closed society or toward a more open one. For example, he has observed that there is a movement toward a more closed society which is characterized by the amount of rage in this country; it seems that everyone is angry with someone else or feels victimized or out of control. As a result, there are many who would like to drive us back to an era that was even less tolerant of individual differences and unresponsive to minority points of view.

Theobald believes that the "gridlock" in this country which was talked about so extensively in the 1992 presidential campaigns is cultural rather than political. The cultural gridlock, symbolized by the emergence of hundreds of vocal minority groups, has led to an era in which more small groups of people demand their rights under the law. There is in turn more backlash which leads to attempts to suppress those rights in favor of the rights of other groups or individuals. Hence, we also face a type of political paralysis because it becomes impossible to reach consensus on any issue.

Furthermore, Theobald has identified four driving principles of this society which must be reexamined. First is the principle of full employment and maximum labor force involvement. The world has been in an economic recession for several years, and most politicians are running their campaigns on the platform of economic development, which equals job creation. However, the statistics are not changing: at least seven percent or more of those eligible to enter the work force are unable to find employment. That statistic may also be misleading because it is based on the number of individuals looking for work, not the total number eligible who have grown discouraged and have stopped looking. Almost every community in this country has a story of some major employer in the area laying off people, or shutting down completely, thereby permanently eliminating jobs. As a result, consumption of goods, which is the second thing identified by Theobald as being a cornerstone of our present society, is also declining. The "consumer confidence" statistic measured by the government fluctuates from month to month but has generally headed downward for quite some time. The dilemma is obvious: if consumers do not consume, then manufacturers need not manufacture, which means that employment of a maximum number of citizens is impossible to achieve.

This dilemma has led to the third thing which Theobald believes is driving this society: specialized education and an enchantment with technology. Our schools are geared more and more to train individuals to fill jobs which are believed to be either presently available or necessary in the future, and the more that training involves the mastery of some advanced form of technology, the more valuable we believe it might be. There seems to be some kind of "high tech" mantra that educators and economists chant these days as though it will solve the employment problems, which will then solve the consumer problem.

Finally, when all else fails, we have turned in this culture to the one sure way to gear up the economy and the fourth identified driving social force: war. Shooting at people who live in other countries has historically been good for business in America, so it is always a tempting solution to an economic problem which continues to defy solution.

Instead of relying on the four principles just discussed, Theobald would have us look in different directions and pay more attention to the counter forces, including a strong antiwar movement and the equally strong environmental movement. Both are collective reactions to the failures of governments to address societal problems in a creative and affirming way. For example, one basis of the antiwar movement has been that destroying people and other governments is a short-term, negative solution to a long term problem. In the same vein, environmentalists have argued for years that destroying nature and consuming natural resources which may not be renewable is the epitome of human arrogance because we continually sacrifice a relationship with nature in order to satisfy short term and limited economic gains.

Both movements, however, are also part of what Theobald would consider a better approach to the future, one which would lead to a more open society as opposed to the closed society which is seen as the only other choice. Instead of trying to perpetuate all the characteristics of the Industrial Era, we need to shift to another paradigm, or way of thinking about society. He calls this new era the Compassionate Era because it is based on the principle of relationships between and among individuals. In that there are no institutions, including governments, which are designed to create change to move us into the future, we have to make it happen locally at the relationship level. Change cannot happen at the traditional "power" level any more. Furthermore, he believes that we are not educating people for the world in which they will live. To face the uncertainties of the future we will need more generalists than specialists, for example. Since computers will handle the specialized information, we will need people to be able to use good judgment, implying that people will need to be solidly grounded in a wide variety of information and knowledge.

In addition, we will need to change our expectations of government. At this time, the federal government is involved in many aspects of life because people at the local level have been unwilling to tackle the tough issues such as racism, classism and ageism. We may have reached the point where the classic battle between "liberals" advocating government involvement in social issues and "conservatives" who want to minimize the government role in people's lives will have to be resolved for these barriers to be removed from peoples' lives. It is going to take individuals and small communities of individuals working together to talk about how to do things without creating dependencies on the government agencies. We must move from our "rights" culture which has fragmented everything to the point where it cannot be dealt with nationally to a "rights with responsibilities" orientation so that problems *can* be solved—at least locally.

Theobald believes that we must encourage creative thinking, and we must make sure that healthy and equal relationships are at the center of all we do. He suggests that we see values as compasses and not as anchors, that we try to understand that people will always behave in their own self-interests but must learn to control their ego needs and behave maturely, and that we accept that everything is connected. If we can think in these ways, then we will be able to change things locally and deal with the radical uncertainties of the future.

In Theobald's view, fundamental change will not occur until people at all levels of society turn away from a dependence on government and turn toward their own communities and local connections to create the worlds in which they wish to live. It will mean facing some very difficult issues and coming to accept that there may no longer be only one definition of reality. It will mean the sharing of power and the honest assessment of every institution we have created. Whether or not we are up to it remains to be seen. The only certainty for Theobald and many other futurists is that if we don't do something, we will be, in a global sense, erecting the railroad crossing sign *after* the wreck has occurred.

Even if one doesn't entirely agree with the world view as expressed by Robert Theobald, there can be no doubt that the world is changing faster than most of us imagine. There is also no doubt that the community colleges many of us are trying to lead into this uncertain future must be poised to abandon ways which no longer work and embrace new strategies which will help us fulfill our mission of providing education to those who need it.

THE FUTURE OF COMMUNITY COLLEGES

President Al Lorenzo of Macomb Community College in Michigan has done much thinking and writing about the future specifically as it pertains to the community college and to the role of the community college president. He has noted changes which have occurred in the planning and organizational characteristics of community colleges in the past thirty years.

For example, he notes that the organizational characteristics and conditions which typified the community college from the 1960s through the early 1980s include the following:

- Rapid growth and development

- Internally directed activity

- An incremental resource base

- Structural simplicity

- Product based and employee centered

- A natural vitality

- Similarity among institutions

However, the attributes which have more recently characterized community colleges have changed rather dramatically, according to Lorenzo. Community colleges are now characterized by:

- Stability and maturity

- Strong external influences

- Often severe resource limitations

- More structural complexity

- Needs based and customer centered

- A sometimes hostile environment

- A general complacency or malaise

- Institutional uniqueness

As a result of these changes, the focus of most institutions has also shifted to issues such as responding to student diversity; adjusting to our resource limitations; refining the curricula; installing technology; initiating partnerships with other social agencies and educational entities; measuring student performance; doing things to enhance our reputations, and helping to develop the communities in which we are located.

Nonetheless, the future is still totally unknown; even while we are engaged in these now familiar activities, we will still be exploring because of one profound difference. Up to now we have lived in a world of rapid change, which has been linear and which required us simply to move faster to keep up. The future, however, is becoming more characterized by radical, non-linear change which can have an instant impact because it implies changing rules and standards. Going faster simply will not work anymore; therefore, our strategies and thinking processes must reflect the ability to deal with radical change and our leadership must be carried out against the backdrop of the emerging contexts of society.

What does this mean? As stated by Lorenzo, it means that while long range thinking is still important, long-range planning can be a trap. It means that organizational speed, flexibility, and responsiveness are now more important to CEO's. And it means that quick response capability in pursuit of a well-articulated vision is preferred over long term planning. It means that the rules and policies which in the past have been the timeless benchmarks to control or predict organizational behavior can now only be temporary and *ad hoc*. If Lorenzo and others who share his views are correct, we can already predict the discomfort that will be felt in institutions which have spent the past thirty years developing policies and procedures to provide direction for the institution. This thinking could wreak havoc on state agencies and boards which try to control us, on collective bargaining unions which often force us into the mediocrity of sameness in the name of equity, and on accrediting bodies which measure quality of educational experience on dangerously outmoded concepts and assumptions.

Lorenzo's prediction is that community colleges will become as diverse as their communities; that what is considered progress on one campus may not be a sign of progress on another; that community colleges will need more situational strategies and fewer inflexible "plans"; and that the community college motto of the future may become "Designed to be Different." Indeed, when we look at just some of the issues we are facing, it becomes apparent that community colleges, as demographic reflections of the communities in which they are located, have some challenging times ahead of them. Every social issue becomes our issue; every educational issue becomes our issue; every economic issue becomes our issue; and every political issue becomes our issue. To state that community college leaders of the future will have to be "pathfinders" borders on the dramatic understatement.

What Will be Considered Effective Leadership?

The question that remains, then, is how to identify those who have the best chance of successfully leading the community college of the future, insofar as we can understand it at this moment. In general, the literature on leadership recognizes the radically changing nature of the world by concluding, for example, that leaders of the future will have to be creative and intuitive (Nanus, 1989); that they will have to be optimists with solid high morale (Gardner, 1990); that leaders must have impeccable ethical standards (Vaughan, 1992); and that leadership styles will have to be based on skills and knowledge rather than on manipulation and power (Theobald, 1992).

Fifty community college presidents gathered together in the summer of 1993 at the Summer Workshop sponsored by AACC's President's Academy were asked to discuss the most important skills, characteristics, or attributes that will be needed by a community college president in the next ten years. It was agreed that there was some overlap between skills and characteristics, but the two lists were separated, and the list of skills is as follows:

1. One of the most important skills that future presidents need for the future is *communication skills*: the ability to listen, the ability to write, and the ability to speak. In addition, effective presidents will also need to have good research skills, and the ability to make good hiring decisions. All of these are part of that umbrella skill of communication.

2. Although the ability to *manage resources* has always been a requisite skill for a leader, community college presidents of the future will need exceptional skill in this area for several reasons: the flow of income to the institution will continue to be less than the demand for expenditures; the demand for technology, both to educate students and to run the organization, will reduce the resources we have to spend in other areas; and the competition for resources will take more of a president's time since constant sources of funds have virtually disappeared. Therefore, it will be critical for a president to be a good scavenger, a talented fund raiser, and a skilled marketer of the institution.

3. In that the amount of information which is available is doubling almost monthly, a successful president will have to be one who is skilled at *sorting and interpreting*, knowing what to discard as irrelevant, what to share with others in the organization, and what to watch for to identify trends which may have an impact.

4. Given the rapid changes in technology, a president will have to be *technologically literate* in order to serve as a facilitator in campus and community discussions about the shape of the future.

5. A president will need *good "people skills"*: conflict resolution abilities,

team building skills to enable people to work together more effectively, and the capacity to envision and create innovative organizational structures which are flexible enough to respond to rapid as well as radical change.

6. Effective presidents will have to have a *global orientation* in their thinking: community colleges may be serving the local community, but that community no longer has the luxury of remaining isolated from the rest of the world, no matter how rural the college.

7. Related to that global orientation will be the necessity for a president to be sensitive to *issues of cultural and economic diversity*, and one strong recommendation is for all presidents of the future to be at least bilingual.

8. Although there are obviously many more skills that could be put on this type of list, one of the most important may be that the president of the future will have to be a *generalist* and a *holistic thinker*. Expertise in one's teaching field or in one area of institutional functioning is no longer going to be enough. We are all going to need to know a lot about a lot in order to keep track of the constantly shifting realities of life.

Closely related to the skills which were seen as being imperative for effective community college presidents were the many characteristics or attributes which were also deemed to be imperative, at least in some combination, in a successful community college president of the future. The following represents the unabridged list of characteristics that the fifty presidents discussed:

integrity	empathetic	high energy level
risk-taker	credible	idealistic
sense of humor	forthright	resourceful
tenacity	persistent	intelligent
courageous realist	self reliant	open-minded
tolerance for ambiguity	self directed learner	flexible
good judgment	life long learner	focused
creative	multi-talented	visionary
humanist	persuasive	student centered
calm under fire	committed	willing to share
centered	honest	governance
adaptive	patient	catalyst for commu-
affinity for change	enthusiastic	nity change

One characteristic mentioned by a president who is Navajo is called "kai," a concept connoting friendship and respect, the basic elements of relationships. His college and his leadership style is grounded in "kai", which was understood and agreed with even though it probably was never pronounced properly.

In 1988, Lawrence Keller completed his dissertation study at the University of Arkansas on "Competencies of Future Community College Presidents: Perceptions of Selected Community College Presidents". He used the Delphi method for his study (developing an initial list of competencies, selecting a Delphi panel, administering three questionnaires, and analyzing the data). The panel reached consensus on 41 of 43 competencies which had been identified, and those 41 were then listed in rank order as determined by the third and final response of the panel (which consisted of twenty-seven community college presidents as identified in the 1986 AACJC membership directory). The five competencies in which there was no standard deviation were *Delegation* ("the ability to know when, when not, and how to assign tasks to others including the ability to grant necessary authority to others and hold them accountable"); *Personnel Selection* ("the ability to attract and select quality people"); *Judgment* ("the ability to choose effectively among courses of alternative action. Includes the ability and willingness to establish priorities."); *Commitment* ("the ability to demonstrate and communicate commitment to a course of action, principle or institution."); and *Decision-Making* (no definition provided). The other competencies, listed in their rank order included:

Interpersonal Skills	Organizing	Controlling
Integrity	Information Processing	Introspection
Knowledge of Mission	Public Relations	Patience
Commitment to Mission	Entrepreneurship	Charisma
Motivation	Finance/Budgeting	Peer Network
Communication	Risk Taking	Scholarly Writing
Flexibility	Emotional Balance/Control	
Leadership	Time Management	
Positive Attitude	Integrating	
Energy	Conflict Resolution	
Wellness	Performance Appraisal	
Planning	Analysis	
Visionary	Sense of Humor	
Sense of Responsibility	Research	
Persistence	Creativity/Innovation	
Use of Power	Empathy	

were also mentioned at least once by the presidents in 1993, but based on the discussions that accompanied the items, one would conclude that the competencies would be ranked differently in 1993 than they were in 1988. For example, the management of resources is a broader approach to finance and budgeting concerns and could be a reflection of the financing crises faced by most public institutions since 1989. We have gone beyond needing to know how to manage budgets to needing to know how to manage and develop resources, and we now expect that this particular economic cycle is going to be "permanent." In addition, risk-taking would probably rate a higher placement on the list, as would conflict resolution, creativity/innovation, and communication. Perhaps the conclusion is that the basic understanding of what it takes to be an effective community college president has not changed, but that the relative importance of the various competencies shifts with time and depends on the external forces shaping our institutions.

We also react to the experiences we have just survived. By far the most dramatic shift that has occurred in the last five years starts with declining resources and gets translated into needing to make sure we communicate well since everyone is on edge, into concentrating on our relationships within the institution since scarcity brings out the worst tendencies in human nature, and into flexibility since efficiency and being able to shift directions quickly to meet student and community needs is what will determine which institutions thrive and which ones merely survive.

PRESIDENTIAL LEADERSHIP FOR THE FUTURE

The fifty presidents who gathered together in the summer of 1993 to discuss the community college of the future also identified a number of issues of which they believe community college presidents must be cognizant in order to provide effective leadership. Those issues included:

1. Organizing and delivering services in new forms in order to respond to issues of student diversity, resource scarcity, local economic development needs, and the availability of different technologies.

2. Developing new roles for faculty in light of the above statement, as well as in relationship to applications of new technologies and collaborations with other agencies.

3. Determining the college's role in social issues.

4. Understanding the teaching/learning process in a new environment and being able to focus on outcomes.

5. Being responsive to but not totally controlled by external pressures

which attempt to dictate access or mission.

6. Knowing what role to play in the formulation of public policies.

7. Understanding the true impact of globalization.

8. Achieving a true customer orientation.

Obviously these are not the only issues being faced— there are always more issues than we have energy to think about at one time. However, these eight items do represent the categories which will likely dominate the community college president's agenda: issues involving people, issues involving the continued advances in technology, and issues involving structure.

People Issues

In a 1993 *Community College Journal* article, Beverly S. Simone, president and district director of Madison Area Technical College and immediate past president of the Board of Directors of AACC, discussed how presidents go about creating climates for change by recognizing the types of people who work in most organizations and by making sure that our behaviors as president "model respect for every individual within our institutions....promote individual autonomy and nurture connections.... and empower every individual within the college." (p. 3) Obviously that is much easier said than done. Her point, however, is that we will not be able to face this radically changing environment in which we are supposed to be educating students for their futures if we are not able, as institutions, to face change ourselves. It is the president who will, according to Simone, be the facilitator of change and the builder of the human resources needed to accomplish our educational tasks. Thus the president of the future will have to have "people skills" and will have to believe in empowerment of individuals and groups within the organization. Traditional hierarchies and organizational charts showing neatly lined relationships within various parts of the organization may become archived as colorful relics of the institution's past.

Technology Issues

Zelema Harris, president of Parkland College in Champaign, Illinois, states that as CEO's we must find ways to make sure that technology is serving all students. We must show that technology is not a tool of the elite and powerful, but that it is something to be used by everyone. In her view, visionary leadership is that which matches technology with human needs and which helps to create socially oriented technology policies. She points out that as a whole, community colleges are medium-level users of information technology. Technology is primarily being used to create databases, support distance learning, provide multimedia options for instruction, and to network. However, she also points out that by the year 2005, the demand in the workplace for systems analysts and computer programmers will increase by seven percent, while by the year 2000 eighty percent of the manual skills jobs we now have will be eliminated. Those statistics also lead to another question about middle management and whether or not that level of the organization has outlived its usefulness. In other words, if the role of a middle manager is to process information, then cannot that role be fulfilled by computers? Applying that concept to the community college, then, Harris speculates that the presidents of the future must not only make sure that all students have access to technology, but that they must also rethink how managers are being utilized as a result of the higher levels of technology in the institution. If we don't need managers to process information because that is being done technologically, then perhaps we can utilize them more to improve the teaching and learning process.

According to Harris, the top information technology concerns in higher education are networking and coping with limited resources. Over three billion dollars were spent in 1992 on education computer products, a staggering sum especially when one puts it in the context of the overall decline in resources in the last five years. Therefore, as presidents we must make sure that money is being spent on what will give our institutions the most pay back. That means that presidents must be computer literate and understand the implications of technology, both on the organization and on the delivery of instruction. Thus, the building projects of the future for presidents may not be classrooms to house more students on campus, but rather computer and media networks that will provide more ways for students to learn at home.

Structural Issues

While the world is being turned on its ear with the radical changes brought about by information technology, at the same time the president still has to manage and lead the organization: to know how to continue its development, how to manage its inevitable change, and how to measure its effectiveness. Total quality management has been one of the most widely adopted strategies for helping business and industry face the future with more effectiveness and more efficiency. Of late, that movement has been translated to a concept of "continuous quality assurance" for the community college, according to Clifford Peterson, president of Quinsigamond Community College in Worcester, Massachusetts. Peterson calls it a decision-making strategy which for his campus has led to two key components:

the continued development and assessment of outcomes for every work unit of the college, and individual employee improvement because outcomes are defined and ways of measuring those outcomes are delineated. He says that they are also getting a great deal of positive information about the college which can be used in all kinds of ways because they have moved from analysis only to plans for improvement of identified weaknesses or concerns. In his view, the president acts as the chief quality officer and as such reflects an attitude more than a management style. As one who has been a president for a very long time, Peterson is convinced that the effective president of the future is going to have to adopt the continuous quality perspective in order to help the institution adapt to and prepare for the challenges of the future.

It is unlikely that future presidents will possess all of the skills or characteristics identified here. However, if we can make some generalizations from the week's discussions, we would have to say that there were basic themes or patterns in those characteristics and skills in spite of seeming contradictions in individual items. Community college presidents, in order to be effective leaders and managers of their institutions, are going to have to be more flexible than in the past, more inclusive in their decision-making, more concerned with relationships within the organization and less concerned with power and structure, and more willing to be a visible leader for community change. In addition, the president will have to be intelligent, articulate, and capable of inspiring students and staff to achieve up to their full potential while embracing their common purpose. For all of us who have said we wanted to "make a difference," I don't yet know how many of us can clearly answer the question, "Difference in what?" Being able to answer *that* question may be the key to preparedness for this job.

According to the report, *An American Imperative*, (1993), the future includes a country which is facing a crisis of values in addition to everything else that is changing so radically. American higher education, including community colleges, must find a way to respond to that crisis by "taking values seriously," by "putting student learning first," and by "creating a nation of learners." There is a growing public concern that higher education is too expensive, is not producing a truly educated populace ready to face the challenges of an increasingly complex society, and is both inefficient and set in its ways. Even though in community colleges we believe that we are not like the colleges and universities who are "guilty" of such crimes, we must not be too smug about our track record. Most of all, anyone who is or wants to be a community college president must take the public concern about the decline in the quality of education as a personal challenge. We have continually to question what we are doing, how we are doing it, and why we are doing it, or we will also be buried by the events of history. And perhaps rightly so.

These are noble statements meant to inspire rather than to discourage, to energize not to burden. This is not an easy life, nor will it be getting any easier. The responsibilities are growing as community colleges take their rightful place leading social change and preparing students for their futures. There are tremendous personal rewards in watching others succeed because of something we have had a part in creating. Perhaps that is the "making a difference" that my colleagues keep mentioning as a prime motivator in their decisions to become community college presidents. My hope is that each of us is not only making a difference, but that we are also preparing the path for the leaders of the future so that they will be even better presidents and more effective leaders for their generation.

References

American Council on Education. *Higher Education Today: Facts in Brief.* Washington, D.C., 1992.

American Council on Education. *A Blueprint for Leadership: How Women College and University Presidents Can Shape the Future.* Washington, D.C., 1994.

Argyris, Chris and Richard Cyert. *Leadership in the 80's: Essays on Higher Education.* Cambridge, MA: Harvard University Institute for Institutional Management, 1980.

Bennis, Warren and Burt Nanus. *Leaders: The Strategies for Taking Charge.* New York, NY: Harper and Row, 1985.

Birnbaum, Robert. *How Academic Leadership Works.* San Francisco, CA: Jossey-Bass, 1992.

Bowen, Howard. *The Costs of Higher Education.* San Francisco, CA: Jossey-Bass, 1980.

Brenneman, David and Susan Nelson. *Financing Community Colleges: An Economic Perspective.* Washington, DC: The Brookings Institution, 1981.

Chait, Richard. "Colleges Should Not be Blinded by Vision." *The Chronicle of Higher Education.* Vol. 40, p. B1-2, Sept. 22, 1993.

Dilenschneider, Robert L. *A Briefing for Leaders: Communication as the Ultimate Exercise of Power.* New York, NY: HarperCollins, 1992.

Elsner, Paul. "Advice to CEO's: Why Board Relationships Might Break Down." *Trustee Quarterly.* Washington, DC: Association of Community Colleges, Winter, 1993.

Edgerton, Russell. "The Tasks Faculty Perform." *Change,* July/August, 1993, pp. 4-6

Gardner, John W. *Tasks of Leadership.* Washington, DC: Leadership Studies Program, Independent Sector, 1986.

Gilligan, Carol. *In a Different Voice.* Cambridge, MA: Harvard University Press, 1982.

Glenny, Lyman. "The Changing Relations Between Higher Education and Government: Budgeting Practices and Pitfalls." Denver, CO: Education Commission of the States, 1977.

Green, Madelaine F. *Leaders For a New Era: Strategies for Higher Education.* New York, NY: Macmillan, 1988.

Hagberg, Janet. *Real Power: The Stages of Personal Power in Organizations.* Minneapolis, MN: Winston, 1984.

Helgesen, Sally. *The Female Advantage: Women's Ways of Leadership.* New York, NY: Doubleday/Currency, 1990.

Hunt, David E. and Edmund Sullivan. *Between Psychology and Education.* New York, NY: Dryden, 1974.

Kerr, Clark, and Marion L. Gade. *The Many Lives of Academic Presidents.* Washington, D.C.: Association of Governing Boards of Universities and Colleges, 1986.

Lorenzo, Albert L. and William J. Banach. *Critical Issues Facing America's Community Colleges.* Warren, MI: The Institute for Future Studies at Macomb Community College, 1992, 1994.

————*Toward a New Model for Thinking and Planning.* Warren, MI: The Institute for Future Studies at Macomb Community College, 1992.

Mintzberg, Henry. *The Structuring of Organizations.* Englewood Cliffs, NJ: Prentice Hall, 1979.

————. *The Nature of Managerial Work.* New York, New York: HarperCollins Publishers, 1973.

Naisbett, John and Patricia Aburdeen. *Re-inventing the Corporation.* New York, NY: Warner Books, 1985.

Nanus, Burt. *The Leader's Edge: The Seven Keys to Leadership in a Turbulent World.* Chicago, IL: Contemporary Books, 1989.

O'Connell, Thomas E. *Community Colleges: A President's View.* Urbana, IL: University of Illinois Press, 1968.

Peterson, Clifford. *Continuous Quality Assurance: Adapting TQM for Community Colleges.* Washington, D.C.: AACC, 1993.

Roueche, John E., George A. Baker III, and Robert R. Rose. *Shared Vision: Transformational Leadership in American Community Colleges.* Washington, D.C.: The Community College Press, 1989.

Sargent, Alice G. *The Androgynous Manager.* New York, NY: AMACOM, 1981.

Seidman, Earl. *In the Words of the Faculty: Perspectives on Improving Teaching and Educational Quality in Community Colleges.* San Francisco, CA: Jossey-Bass, 1985.

Simone, Beverly. "Creating Climates for Change." *Community College Journal,* 63:3. June/July, 1993.

Theobald, Robert. *The Rapids of Change: Social Entrepreneurship in Turbulent Times.* Indianapolis, IN: Knowledge Systems, Inc., 1987.

————. *Turning the Century.* Indianapolis, IN: Knowledge Systems, Inc., 1992.

Vaughan, George B. *The Community College Presidency.* New York, NY: Macmillan, 1986.

————. *Leadership in Transition: The Community College Presidency.* New York, NY: Macmillan, 1989.

Vaughan, George B. and Associates. *Dilemmas of Leadership: Decision Making and Ethics in the Community College.* San Francisco, CA: Jossey-Bass, 1992.

Wheatley, Margaret. *Leadership and the New Science.* San Francisco, CA: Berrett Koehler, 1992.